IRAQ, INC.
A PROFITABLE OCCUPATION

IRAQ, INC.
A PROFITABLE OCCUPATION

PRATAP CHATTERJEE

An Open Media Book

SEVEN STORIES PRESS
NEW YORK

Seven Stories Press
140 Watts Street
New York, NY 10013
www.sevenstories.com

In Canada: Publishers Group Canada, 250A Carlton Street,
Toronto, ON M5A-2L1

In the U.K.:
Turnaround Publisher Services Ltd., Unit 3, Olympia Trading
Estate, Coburg Road, Wood Green, London N22 6TZ

In Australia:
Palgrave Macmillan, 627 Chapel Street, South Yarra VIC 3141

College professors may order examination copies of Seven Stories
Press titles for a free six-month trial period. To order, visit
www.sevenstories.com/textbook, or fax on school letterhead to
(212) 226-1411.

Book and cover design by Jon Gilbert
Cover photo: Getty Images

9 8 7 6 5 4 3 2 1

Printed in Canada

Contents

....

Introduction

·······

April 9, 2004: On every minaret, a sniper. At every entrance to the mosque, a man with a Kalashnikov. At every alley abutting the Sheraton, a tank. On the first anniversary of the liberation of Iraq the streets appear deserted of civilians. Four neighborhoods of Baghdad are witnessing fierce street battles, the Marines have surrounded Fallujah, and Moqtada al Sadr's army is controlling half a dozen cities in the south.

I made my way though the maze of the hotel zone, threading around the triple rows of concertina wire and the Humvees racing up and down the Tigris. At the side of the road, U.S. soldiers crept along the grassy banks like they'd learned war from an action movie. Arriving at the mosque, I joined the long line of worshippers waiting to be searched, in this case, twice as thoroughly as at any American check-point. Then a vehicle appeared and my party was swiftly ushered past the crowds flocking for Friday afternoon prayers. "*Sahafin, sahafin!*" we would shout ("Journalist, journalist!"), the magic word that would cause every face to smile in welcome.

There weren't many of us. Al Jazeera and Al Arabiya, two popular Arab stations, and myself. No CNN, no BBC, just one white photographer. Uneasily, I took a position on a wall above the moat, fearing that I might fall backwards into the green water, camera and all.

As the imam finished his sermon, tens of thousands spilled out of the Um al Qora mosque, the biggest Sunni mosque in Baghdad. I was swept up in the crowds and lifted on top of a van from which I could see all the way to the entrance—it seemed the best view in town. Three young boys held down the legs of my tripod and another held out the shotgun microphone.

Below me an American flag appeared and a shout went up through the crowd. Looking back through the tapes, the scene seems almost like a gang war, the group of angry young men tearing the flag apart and finally setting it alight. A cry went up, *"Arsh, Arsh Moqtada! Arsh, Arsh Moqtada!"* ("Long live Moqtada!"), destined to send a chill into the hearts of every American soldier. At this Sunni mosque, every man was cheering wildly for a radical Shia cleric.

From every wall, it seemed, a young man would sing into the crowd in call and response. *"Jihad, Jihad, Jihad."* The corners of the mosque were piled high with food, oil, and water waiting to be carried to the *mujahideen* (holy warriors), as they are already being called. Money piled high into the white sacks at the entrance to be sent to the resistance. "The Iraqi *intifada* has begun," said one observer.[1]

I returned to my room on the sixth floor of the Al Fanar hotel. Three doors down from me, a young man by the name of Nicholas Berg sat at a round glass-top coffee table and drank a beer with my neighbor, Andrew Robert Duke. The next morning he checked out and disappeared. He had arrived the day after me, traveling from the north as I did. He had spent a scant four days in the hotel and was never heard from alive again. Over a month later, his decapitated body was found near a highway.[2]

Berg was an idealistic man, by all accounts, who wanted to help Iraq and hoped to set aside some money in the process. Alas, he was in the wrong place at the wrong time, and his tale corresponds, in part, to those of thousands of other earnest Americans who are now living in Iraq, and tens of thousands of unwilling soldiers who had been ordered to protect them while the powers that be in Washington rolled the dice in an economic and military experiment that has failed to make good on their promises. And indeed, taking the architects of the plan at their word, they had promised a lot. Regardless of the international debacle the decision to go to war had been, the administration vowed to transform what critics and a majority of Iraqis had deemed an occupation into liberation.

Just two weeks prior, in anticipation of the one-year anniversary, Paul Bremer delivered a laudatory state of the nation speech at the Baghdad City Council:

> At liberation, this great country had been reduced to a shell, not by war, not by invasion, but by almost four decades of relentless greed and cruelty by its leaders. Instead of investing in Iraq's infrastructure, Saddam's regime squandered and stole the nation's wealth. Instead of serving his citizens Saddam deprived them of access to essential services. When liberation came, water, electricity, sewage, schools and much more were a shambles. When liberation came, not a single policeman was on duty in Iraq and the Army had disappeared.

What a difference a year can make in the life of the Iraqi people.

➤ Today over 200,000 Iraqis are serving in Iraq's security forces protecting Iraq, its people and infrastructure.

➤ Today Iraq has more electrical power than before liberation. And more is coming.

➤ Already more than 2,500 schools have been rehabilitated by the Coalition.

➤ Over 3 million Iraqi children under five have been vaccinated against polio and other diseases.

➤ The Coalition has increased health care spending by more than thirty times and it is still growing.

➤ Since May, the Coalition has completed almost eighteen thousand individual reconstruction projects across the length and breadth of the country.

➤ The economy is picking up steam. And indicators are that unemployment is half what it was at liberation—and possibly below what is was before the war.

➤ Iraq's new currency has gained 29 percent since it was introduced just a few months ago.

➤ Today over one million Iraqis enjoy telephone service—more than before the war. And that number grows by 15,000 per week.

➤ Iraq is once again a member of the international community, routinely joining sister states in the Arab League, the United Nations, the World Bank and IMF.

➤ And, in an area where I am particularly happy to report, after over five hundred elections at sports clubs all over the country, Iraq is again a member of the International Olympic Committee. And this summer in Athens Iraqi athletes will compete under the Iraqi flag at the Olympics.

But the great achievement of Iraq is in the political area. Iraq is now on a path to full democracy in a united state at peace with its neighbors.[3]

From the streets of Baghdad, gridlocked by day for want of traffic police, dark by nightfall for lack of electricity, and always overflowing with garbage, I wondered how Bremer and I could see such radically different Iraqs.

The patina on the occupation official's speech dulled when one examined the details or simply looked to the streets. According to official accounts, the administration had fallen far short of its stated commitment that Bremer had parroted to the council. At a House Appropriations Committee hearing in late April 2004 it was revealed that less than 5 percent of the $18.4 billion earmarked in fiscal 2003 for the reconstruction of Iraq had actually been spent. (When I spoke to Luke Zahner, an official at the United States Agency for International Development [USAID], he contradicted this report, saying that his agency alone had spent some $1.5 billion—what amounts to a slim 8 percent of the total.) Just $2.3 billion had been allocated to projects through March 24, 2004 and only $1 billion had been spent.[4]

The details were even more embarrassing: occupation officials reassigned $184 million appropriated for drinking-water projects to fund the operations of the new U.S. Embassy, while $29 million was moved from projects such as "democracy building" to pay for administrative expenses. Of the $279 million earmarked for irrigation projects, for instance, none had been spent nor had the $152 million allocated for dam repair and construction. The occupation authorities had set aside $240 million for road and bridge construction, of which only $20 million had been spent.[5]

Another report, from the Pentagon's program management office in Baghdad released in mid-May 2004, reported that just 24,179 Iraqis were employed in rebuilding projects, that is, less than one percent of Iraq's work force of more than 7 million. Of Halliburton's twenty-four thousand employees, just one in four were Iraqi citizens. "Iraqis are thinking twice about working for the Americans because of the latest violence, which has targeted not only U.S. troops but also Iraqis working with them," writes Associated Press reporter Matt Kelley. "The latest fighting not only prevented work on current projects but hampered future efforts by delaying the arrival of coalition equipment and manpower," concludes the reporter.[6]

Yet occupation authorities relentlessly focused on positive news, such as highly unlikely employment statistics. "Now, the Ministry of Planning has released a 28 percent number, which conforms with two CPA numbers that put unemployment [rates] in the mid-20s. It's still way too high, but it's better than it was, and it seems to be moving in the right direction," said Bremer staffer Thomas Foley, before he quit his job.[7] Yet, by way of comparison, six months prior, the Labor Ministry estimated that 70 percent of the Iraqi population was without jobs.[8] From where these new jobs Foley spoke of had appeared was incomprehensible, since the occupation did not appear to be a significant employer of Iraqis.

"At a time when more and more of the Iraqi people are losing faith in our good intentions," said Nita Lowe, the ranking Democrat on the House Appropriations Foreign

Operations Subcommittee, "this is a good indication of how few average Iraqis are seeing the benefits of reconstruction. More Iraqis clearly should be benefiting from the reconstruction efforts."[9]

What went wrong?

I traveled to the region four times in the last three years to find out.

Within days of the fall of Baghdad, thousands of local and expatriate contractors, working for multinational corporations, were hired to reconstruct the country and install democracy at a profit that most assumed would be paid for from Iraq's vast oil wealth.

But the oil did not flow as quickly as expected and the companies failed to make good on their promises, so within months the security situation deteriorated, bringing yet another wave of fortune seekers: the private security companies that cleaned up big by providing security services to the terrified businessmen. Meanwhile the U.S. government and army, afraid to demoralize their troops, hired foreign sweatshop labor to do every menial task from cleaning toilets to guard duty, increasing the anger of ordinary Iraqis, three out of every four of whom had no jobs.

In my conversations with Iraqis, I was reminded of the time I spent documenting the impact of California's 1849 Gold Rush on Native Americans and also of my visits to the modern-day equivalents of that era, in the present day Philippines and in the Amazon. I witnessed the same frontier mentality in Iraq; here all measure of opportunists hatched get-rich-quick schemes with nary a thought for the local people or the future of the place. Yet that was not the only analogy that sprang to mind. As I visited American bureaucrats in Saddam's old palaces, ministries, and hotels,

I felt as though I were watching old newsreels of colonial British India. And every day as I watched the soldiers driving through town in their armored Humvees and Stryker vehicles, weighed down with the latest in modern war technology, I imagined I was in Nixon's Vietnam.

Historical analogies aside, I believe the situation in Iraq is unique and I leave it to you the reader to decide which, if any, of these analogies apply.

CHAPTER ONE

Operation Sweatshop Iraq

On May 1, 2003, U.S. President George Bush emerged from a plane on the USS *Abraham Lincoln*, anchored just off the coast of San Diego, and strode out to address the admiring crowds under a banner that read "Mission Accomplished." Three weeks later, engineers and executives from San Francisco-based Bechtel, one of the world's largest construction firms, kicked off a road show for companies that wanted to win profitable contracts in the reconstruction of Iraq. The first conference was held a block from the White House at the Ronald Reagan Building on May 21. Two days later, the U.K. Department of Trade and Industry hosted a meeting for the company at the Novotel in Hammersmith in southwest London. On May 28, the tour ended with a stop at the Sheraton hotel in Kuwait City.

From those early meetings to the one-year anniversary of Iraq's "liberation," contracts to rebuild the country would total tens of billions of dollars—the story of which would lead me far from the capitals of Britain and the United States to the streets of Kirkuk, Baghdad, and Basra.

• • •

Red shadows rippled across the desert sand of southern Iraq as gray tendrils of smoke billowed from the sheet of flames dancing bright orange over the twelve outstretched chimneys. It sounded like a jet engine from almost a hundred feet away, and if I looked into the flames I could feel my skin burn. I stepped back, glad of the cool blue sky around me that allowed me to rest my eyes, before I gazed back into the hypnotic fire.

Eventually I tore my gaze away and walked back with Hamid Miala, a foreman for South Oil Company, who has worked here at the Zubair oil fields for twenty-seven years of his life. He was glad to keep his job when Saddam Hussein's government was ousted by the U.S. invasion in the early spring of 2003. Since the invasion his salary had been raised to about two hundred dollars a month, almost five times that of his pay under the Ba'athist regime.

This two hundred dollar paycheck, one of the highest that local workers can earn, was the product of a long, strong union struggle to maintain Iraqi jobs because the occupation authorities prefer to hire foreign workers, despite the fact that they command much higher wages.

Over by the turbines that pump the oil from the wells to the port of Basra, I met a crew of three Indian and Pakistani workers. They were dressed in the blue uniforms of the Al Kharafi Company, a Kuwaiti subcontractor working for Kellogg Brown & Root (KBR), a subsidiary of Halliburton. In 2003, Halliburton won contracts that range from cooking meals, delivering mail, and building bases, to repairing Iraq's oil industry. That year these contracts totaled more than $8 billion.

Abdul Hakim, a crane operator from Lahore, Pakistan, had worked in the Persian Gulf the longest of the three men. After working there for ten years, he and his colleagues earn as much as fifteen hundred dollars a month, seven times more than his Iraqi counterparts. "The company gives us free housing and food and drives us here every day across the border. And I can visit my family in Lahore every year. It's a good job," he said.

As we chatted, we were joined by two Indian workers: Sanjay Singh and Imman Hassan. They had worked in the Gulf for only two years making $550 a month as fabricators, but they came from an army of skilled mechanics shipped to the Middle East from South Asia. "Most of us are Indian—we probably have ten thousand people in Kuwait, but we also have Pakistanis, Bangladeshis and Sri Lankans," said Singh.

I left the oil fields for the nearby city of Basra to meet Hassan Jum'a, the leader of the South Oil Company union. In the neighborhood of Jhoomouria, as I pulled up to a decrepit, crumbling house, I found piles of garbage rotting in the street. Inside I was greeted by pitch darkness, a common occasion in occupied Iraq where Bechtel was struggling to restore full power to the grid.

Jum'a was surprised to hear about our encounter with the South Asian workers; just a few months prior his union staged a wildcat strike to kick out the foreigners. "The policy of our company is to refuse the foreign workers. We prefer to let the Iraqi people do the work. Halliburton agreed to bring a few technicians which they mostly needed. But the workers are Iraqi people," he told us.

He shook his head grimly when I told him what the foreign workers earn. "This is one of the reasons why we refused foreign workers. Because the Iraqi worker will notice a very big gap between his salary and the foreign worker's," he said.

Accompanying me to Jum'a's house was Ewa Jasiewicz, a British temporary worker with Baghdad-based Occupation Watch, who spent three months in Iraq helping the union to organize workers. It proved to be an uphill struggle.

"Most, if not all, the workers we have met so far did not clearly understand what a union was or why it would be in their interest to join one. They did not comprehend union structures, the right to strike, the right of free association and collective bargaining, and the idea of challenging the boss in a sustainable way, rather than just rioting or kicking him," she said.[10]

Saddam Hussein instilled the fear of collective organizing in these workers on March 11, 1987, when he abolished basic rights including the eight-hour day. Saddam's 1987 law axed the right to form or join unions or to bargain. While unions in the public sector were banned, new "unions" were created for the private sector to, according to the law, work with management to "increase efficiency and work discipline."

This law was reaffirmed on June 5, 2003, when Paul Bremer issued a decree called Public Incitement to Violence and Disorder. The edict announced that anyone who "incite(s) civil disorder, rioting or damage to property . . . will be subject to immediate detention by Coalition Provisional Authority security forces and held as a security internee under the Fourth Geneva Convention of 1949 [which governs prisoners of war]." Labor activists say that the phrase "civil disorder" could be used to target people organizing strikes.

Indeed, in early December, a convoy of ten Humvees and armored personnel carriers arrived at the office of the Iraqi

Workers Federation of Trade Unions, whereupon United States soldiers jumped out, stormed the building, and arrested eight members of the federation's executive board.

"They gave no reason at all, despite being asked over and over," said federation spokesperson Abdullah Muhsin Although the eight were released the following day, there was no explanation from the occupation authorities for the detentions. Nor were these the first unionists to be apprehended. Two other trade union leaders—Qasim Hadi, general secretary of the Union of the Unemployed, and Adil Salih, another leader of the organization—were arrested in November.[11]

Across Iraq, workers are facing the same dilemma. Unions have managed to stage strikes to improve pay scales, but workers face arrest or intimidation from the occupation forces. Adding insult to injury is the fact that unionists could lose their jobs to foreign workers who are paid far higher salaries than even the unions are demanding.

In early February the *Wall Street Journal* reported that Halliburton was shipping in five hundred American workers a week, paying four times the amount the same workers could earn in Halliburton's native Texas,[12] offering up to eight thousand dollars a month to drive oil trucks. I asked the oil workers, members of possibly the strongest union in the country, what could be done to protect Iraqi jobs. Jum'a answered simply: "You can't hide the moon: each honest Iraqi should refuse the occupation. Our ambition is for the occupation forces to leave as soon as possible."

HALLIBURTON'S DIRTY DISHES

The week after my trip to the southern oil fields, I traveled north from Basra to Baghdad where I was invited to discuss

Halliburton's military contracts with a U.S. Army spokesperson. Our appointment was at the Al Rasheed hotel, Baghdad's most exclusive, which modestly advertises itself as "more than a hotel." Right after the war in 2003, it became part of the temporary headquarters for the occupation forces in Iraq and, as such, could be approached only by traversing miles of coiled barbed wire, a maze of concrete barricades designed to stop the most determined suicide bomber, and checkpoints run by heavily armed soldiers from the Florida National Guard.

As I entered the Al Zaheer restaurant inside the hotel, I once again encountered South Asians: Muzaffar, a cook from a small village some forty miles from Dhaka, Bangladesh; Shahnawaz, a waiter from Delhi, India; and Ali from the lawless North-West Frontier Province in Pakistan, who worked behind the salad bar.

These men worked quietly together serving meals in the three-hundred-seat dining room. Sprawled out at the tables were uniformed soldiers and Secret Service men with earpieces (guns never more than an arm's length from their reach), smartly dressed secretaries from military contracting firms, and men in dark business suits chatting loudly about the business of running a country.

I was invited to lunch as the guest of Richard Dowling, the spokesperson for the United States Army Corps of Engineers. Dressed in full tan military camouflage uniform, he is a cheerful, middle-aged, white-bearded civilian who had worked for the army for twenty-three years. His sanguine appearance earned him the name Baba Noel, the Arabic translation for Santa Claus. As we lunched, I ate uneasily, remembering an NBC news report stating that the Pentagon repeatedly warned Halliburton that the food it served to U.S.

troops in Iraq was "dirty," as were the kitchens in which it was prepared. The Pentagon reported finding "blood all over the floor," "dirty pans," "dirty grills," "dirty salad bars," and "rotting meats . . . and vegetables" in four of the military messes the company operates in Iraq. Halliburton's promises to improve "have not been followed through," according to the Pentagon report that warned "serious repercussions may result" if the contractor did not clean up.[13]

The meals at the Al Rasheed were mediocre but they were definitely a step up from the Meals-Ready-To-Eat issued to soldiers on the battlefield. Yet, for the kind of cash that the U.S. military was spending (twenty-eight dollars a day, per soldier), soldiers could be eating at the White Palace, one of the best restaurants in Baghdad, fancied by Bremer himself.

After our meal, I stopped to chat with the workers who told me they were earning three hundred dollars a month, including overtime and hazard pay. Asked what they think of their jobs, they are noncommittal. "Chalta he," said one: "We manage somehow." Muzaffar, the cook, explained that it's a lot more than he makes at home. He's paid for his eldest daughter to get married to another Bangladeshi who lives in Saudi Arabia. But both he and his son-in-law rarely get to see their wives. His other daughter and his young son barely know him as he has lived abroad for thirteen years.

While some of the men working for Halliburton in Iraq were recruited to these jobs directly from India by the Saudi-based Tamimi Corporation, most are brought over from Kuwait or Saudi Arabia, where they were offered bonus pay to work in Iraq. One worker says that the company really didn't offer him a choice: it was Iraq or get laid off. These men never left the grounds of the hotel or the Republican

Palace because it was considered far too dangerous to venture out of the high-security Green Zone they said.

Our conversation was cut short by Tony, a Filipino American ex-Marine from Burlingame, California, the man in charge of the sixty South Asian staff. "Back to work," he snarled. "All of you in the kitchen now." As he spoke neither Urdu nor Bengali, our conversation was incomprehensible to him and maybe that made him nervous.

"Tony's such a hard-ass," said Mike, one of the military contractors and witness to the exchange. "Give them a break," he called out, as I rose to leave. The three kitchen workers were apologetic. "Come back to meet us at the palace," they say. "Sometimes we cook Indian food there."

As I left the hotel I asked Dowling about the allegations that Halliburton is profiting from the war in Iraq. "Some may see it as war profiteering, but, for the young soldiers, it is hot food and a dry place to sleep," he explained. "Yes, it is a profit motive that brings companies into a dangerous location, but that is what capitalism is all about. Halliburton employees are under fire and several have died but they are still here. With all due respect to nonprofit organizations like the United Nations and the Red Cross, they have pulled out. If it takes profit to motivate an organization to take a tough job, then that's the only way to do it," he said.

COOKING THE NUMBERS

In December 2003, Halliburton estimated that it had served 21 million meals so far to the 110,000 troops at forty-five sites in Iraq, according to numbers provided by an NBC reporter. But early in 2004, military auditors began to suspect that the company might be cooking the numbers and overcharging the government by millions of dollars.[14]

In February, the *Wall Street Journal* reported that Halliburton might have overcharged taxpayers by more than $16 million for meals served during the first seven months of 2003 to U.S. troops serving in Operation Iraqi Freedom. In July 2003 alone Halliburton billed for 42,042 meals a day but served only 14,053 meals daily.[15]

Melissa Norcross, a spokesperson for Halliburton's Middle East region, defended the company's practices with an explanation from Randy Harl, chief executive officer of Halliburton: "For example, commanders do not want troops 'signing in' for meals due to the concern for safety of the soldiers; nor do they want troops waiting in lines to get fed." Norcross also claimed that the "dirty kitchen" problems have been taken care of, and the facilities have since passed subsequent inspections.

"Keep in mind that serving food to more than 130,000 patrons daily in a hostile war zone is not easy. And it's worth noting that although there are many challenges involved in supplying food to more than 130,000 patrons every day, there are also accounts of wonderful things our employees do," said the Halliburton spokesperson. She quoted a note from a Halliburton client in Tall Afar, Iraq: "The commander gave kudos to staff for the Thanksgiving Meal served. He said it was the best he had ever seen and I told him that it was the best that I have seen anywhere in 23 years of government service."

LOCAL LABOR

I bade farewell to Dowling and walked from the Al Rasheed to the Baghdad convention center, which holds a vast empty theater, but also houses lively offices from the basement to the third floor. Earnest-looking Iraqis, the military and their private guards, and the odd camera crew mostly populated the rooms.

Eventually a group of Iraqi convention center workers, wearing Halliburton badges, stopped by to chat on their tea break. One of them tried to pronounce the word "congratulations" several times but failed. Unable to wish his boss well, he exasperatedly turned to me to ask if there was a better word. I suggested slapping the boss on the back and saying: "Good job! Well done!" but he shook his head violently. "No, I cannot say that—Mr. Lewis is an American, my boss. I must say something more polite."

The three convention hall employees were friends and lived in the same neighborhood. Every morning Halliburton sent a car to pick them up for work at 8:00 A.M., and at 4:00 P.M. a car took them back home. The three were professionals, which are generally better paid by Halliburton than laborers. Khaled Ali was an engineer in charge of construction at the convention center, Saba Adel Mostafa was an interpreter, and Daoud Farrod was a supervisor. Daoud was the eldest, the others in their late twenties. They told me they were excited to work for Halliburton.

"It's my first job. I was not able to practice my English before. And the government pay before was just ten dollars a month," Saba said. Khaled explained that it is his first job too. "And you are in charge of all the construction here?" I asked. He nodded proudly, beaming when I exclaimed, "Congratulations!" The three of them said that Iraqi Halliburton workers earn between one- and three-hundred dollars a month.

TEMPS FROM TEXAS

Half a world away, another group of desperate workers could
be found at recruiting sessions in Houston. Their prospec-
tive employer had posted flyers at truck stops and placed
advertisements on the Internet. Four out of five recruits
invited to training sessions at a defunct Montgomery Ward
store near the Houston airport would be sent to Iraq. In early
January, Halliburton was sending an average of five hundred
recruits a week.

These men were not skilled. "They are unemployed and
underemployed workers with few jobs in a U.S. economy
that isn't producing many jobs," writes Russell Gold, a *Wall
Street Journal* reporter. Gold interviewed men lining up for
the training sessions, citing the example of one typical appli-
cant whose previous job was transporting chickens for
twelve dollars an hour. But when they arrived in Iraq, their
navy blue American passports earned them a tidy sum of
money: between seven- and eight-thousand dollars a month,
generous paychecks even by American standards. In return
they had to work twelve to fifteen hours a day, seven days a
week, often living in tents and subject to blinding sand-
storms, as well as temperatures exceeding 130 degrees.[16]

I asked company spokesperson Norcross about the huge
disparity in wages (based on nationality) that Halliburton
paid in Iraq. "We will not discuss our specific wage structures. Our compensation packages and the compensation
packages provided by our subcontractors are based on a wage
scale that was recommended by the Coalition Provisional
Authority in Iraq, and are competitive in terms of the local
market," she wrote back.[17]

The same question posed to army spokesperson Dowling
yielded a more revealing answer. "These workers consider

themselves fortunate to have jobs even if it means them traveling somewhere else. There is an army of companies that move from conflict to conflict with experience in setting up chow halls from an empty field to a thousand army camps in a matter of days. It's not an easy job and these guys are good at it. They bring their own people with them—people with experience in other military locations," Dowling explained.

"The [salary] decision is not based on the value of his life but on the cost of training and equipping the workforce. Nor would it be right for the U.S. Army to enforce U.S.–based salaries where no one else could match it. Life sometimes isn't fair," he concluded.

WHO'S FAIR AND WHO'S NOT?

But sometimes the unfairness seems to be either unnecessary or deliberate. For example, the complex system of subcontracting that delivers the South Asian cooks to the U.S. military can penalize both the worker and the taxpayer.

The system works as follows: Halliburton hires Tamimi in Saudi Arabia, which may in turn subcontract Gulf Catering in Kuwait, which in turn will use an agent in India, such as Subhash Vijay Associates. As each contractor expects a fee for services, we, the taxpayer, are expected to pay a sum that is several times higher than the worker's three-hundred-dollar-a-month salary.

And the Indian worker may not even get his full share. In early May 2004, a news story surfaced in the Indian press reporting that contractor Subhash Vijay Associates offered Abdul Aziz Hamid and his younger brother Shahjahan, from southern India, two-year contracts to work as butchers on a military base in Kuwait for an eighteen-hundred-dollar fee.

The men were promised salaries of $385 a month, a small fortune by Indian standards, so they mortgaged a relative's house and land, paid the fee, and flew to Kuwait in August with two of their friends. Within days the brothers were taken to a U.S. military base in northern Iraq minus their passports. Their supervisor, who had taken their passports in Kuwait, told them they were required to work on the base for six months and could not leave. Their work consisted of washing dishes and cleaning up after American soldiers for $150 a month. "We were in hell. I told my wife over the phone, 'If God wills us, we will meet again.'"

Nico Smith, personnel manager for Gulf Catering, which employed the men, denied exploiting them. "The passports are only kept for safekeeping. When they wanted to resign we never said they can't go," he told *The New York Times*.

Wendy Hall, a Halliburton spokeswoman, said that the company would aggressively investigate the company. "KBR has a policy to terminate any and all subcontractors if we know of mistreatment of employees. Under KBR policies our employees are allowed to quit and leave the sector at their choosing."[18]

Meanwhile other catering subcontractors claim that Halliburton has been exploiting them—among them the company that provided Thanksgiving dinner to George Bush when he made a surprise visit to Baghdad in 2003, appearing in front of the cameras offering U.S. troops a plastic turkey on a tray.[19] Morris Corporation, an Australian catering company, in partnership with a Kuwaiti company, KCPC, was hired in June 2003 to supply meals to eighteen thousand troops at three bases in northern Iraq for $100 million. Six weeks later Halliburton canceled the contract saying that Morris and its Kuwaiti partner had not fulfilled their obligations. A whistle-blower told the *Sydney Morning Herald* that an American Halliburton employee approached the Australian-Kuwaiti venture during the contract negotiations seeking kickbacks worth up to $3 million. "We're not talking about a paper bag. This guy was after a percentage of your sales every month. They wanted kickbacks of 3 percent to 4 percent, which pushed up the prices because then the sub-contractors would add the price of the kickbacks to their costs."[20]

"COST PLUS" EQUALS BIG PROFITS

Why the reluctance to pay Iraqi workers decent wages and the prohibition of unions, when this could actually be a cost-effective solution to the problem of massive unemployment and the steady demand for reconstruction labor, while soothing the anger that many Iraqis feel about the occupation? The simple answer is that Halliburton and the occupation authorities simply do not trust Iraqi workers, fearing that they might kick out or kill their colonial bosses.

The Halliburton sweatshops that pay $100 a month for locals, $300 for Indians and $8,000 for Texans are like any other industry in the world. Despite common perceptions that sweatshop jobs are the least-liked jobs, in most countries, multinational companies pay little more than local jobs (if they are available), making them attractive to the local population. One hundred dollars is a lot of money in a country with 70 percent unemployment, while $300 is a small fortune in India, and $8,000 is what engineers earn in America. It's no surprise that Halliburton has no shortage of job applicants for the few openings it has.

As Dowling explained, the company is careful not to pay workers too much over the average salary, but ultimately the company does not care how much it spends, because under its contracts, the military pays Halliburton for costs plus a small profit margin of one percent. In addition to its direct costs, Halliburton can bill as cost a percentage of its overhead, all the way up to its Houston head office. Once the work is complete, a committee of military brass determines if Halliburton should get an additional performance bonus of up to 2 percent. In the committee's scoring system, 60 percent of the grade is based on the company's performance, such as adhering to schedule, quality of work, and problem solving, while only 40 percent is based on cost control. Thus the more money the company spends, the more profit it can make, making a mockery of the private sector's highly touted efficiency.

WHISTLE-BLOWERS

Indeed, company whistle-blowers have been coming forward to tell the media and members of Congress about how the company promoted a culture of overspending. Henry Bunting, a Vietnam veteran who worked as a purchasing and planning professional for a number of companies, Halliburton, Hewlett-Packard, Tyco, and the Houston Metropolitan Transit Authority, went to work for Halliburton at the Khalifa resort in Kuwait in early May 2003, staying on until mid-August of that year.

Bunting said he never saw an auditor while he was stationed in Kuwait. And workers were told that if they spoke to an auditor or the media, they would be sent home, he added. Eventually he quit because he was "completely worn out" from working twelve to sixteen hour days, but, as he stresses, he was not fired.[21]

On February 13, Bunting testified before a panel of Senate

Democrats, bringing with him an embroidered orange towel, purchased by Halliburton for an exercise facility for U.S. troops in Baghdad, as evidence of the company's practice of overcharging the taxpayer. Halliburton insisted on buying the embroidered towels for $5 apiece, he said, rather than ordinary towels for $1.60 each.

He described the process by which the towels were purchased:

> There were old quotes for ordinary towels. The MWR (Morale, Welfare, Recreation) manager changed the requisition by requesting upgraded towels with an embroidered MWR Baghdad logo. He insisted on this embroidery, which you can see from this towel. The normal procurement practice should be that if you change the requirements, you re-quote the job. The MWR manager pressured both the Procurement supervisor and manager to place the order without another quote. I advised my supervisor of the situation but resigned before the issue was resolved. I assume the order for embroidered towels was placed without re-quoting.[22]

Senator Richard Durbin, a Democrat from Illinois who was attending the hearing, did a quick calculation by which he estimated that the extra cost for the embroidered towels would have paid for twelve suits of body armor, which a number of soldiers were not provided with when they were sent to Iraq.[23]

According to Bunting and other whistle-blowers who spoke with this author on condition of anonymity, Halliburton routinely insisted that the buyers use suppliers that had worked for them in the past, even if they weren't the cheapest. While it is common for companies to use reliable suppliers rather than the cheapest provider, the buyers quickly discovered that the suppliers weren't reliable. "Often these were favors to suppliers that Halliburton had used in Bosnia," one whistle-blower stated.

Bunting explained to senators how the system worked and how the company ripped off the taxpayer.

There are three levels of procurement staffing at Halliburton. Buyers are responsible for ordering materials to fill requisitions from Halliburton employees. We would find a vendor who could provide the needed item and prepare a purchase order. Procurement Supervisors were responsible for the day-to-day operation of the Procurement section. The Procurement, Materials & Property Manager was a step above them.

A list of suppliers was provided by the Procurement supervisor. It was just a list of names with addresses and telephone number. We were instructed to use this preferred supplier list to fill requisitions. As suppliers were contacted, commodities/product information was added. However, we found out over time that many of the suppliers were noncompetitive in pricing, late quoting, and even later in delivery.

While working at Halliburton, I observed several problematic business practices. For purchase orders under $2,500, buyers only needed to solicit one quote from one vendor. To avoid competitive bidding, requisitions were quoted individually and later combined into purchase orders under $2,500. About 70 to 75 percent of the requisitions processed ended up being under $2,500. Requisitions were split to avoid having to get two quotes. For purchase orders above $2,500, buyers were required to obtain two quotes. The buyer would select a high-quoting supplier and a more moderate preferred-quoting supplier. Thus, the buyer would be able to place the purchase order with a preferred supplier, as he or she knew that the quote submitted by the preferred supplier would be lower.

Let me go through a few examples of Halliburton practices....

Because of the influx of people [at Halliburton], the demand for office chairs and desks was high. The preferred supplier had provided office furniture almost from the beginning of Halliburton's time in Kuwait. No one questioned pricing. We simply called, furniture was delivered, and paperwork was completed. The comment by both Halliburton buyers and management was "it's cost plus, don't waste your time finding another supplier." Most requirements for office furniture were filled without competitive quotes.

I took it upon myself to find a second source for the furniture requirement. I received quotes from several suppliers resulting in cost savings of $30 per office desk and $10 per office chair. I estimate these savings as $5,000 to $6,000 per year. The point is that competitive pricing is available in Kuwait. But the preferred supplier list is questionable. Halliburton could reduce costs.[24]

In response to Bunting's charges, Halliburton spokeswoman Cathy Gist defended the company to the media, saying that although the company had requested the towels, they cost three dollars each and were embroidered in an attempt to prevent pilferage.

In June 2003, another group of whistle blowers came forward to testify before the Government Reform Committee at the House of Representatives, but the committee chairman, Tom Davis, a Republican from Virginia, refused to allow them to speak. Representative Henry Waxman, a California Democrat who was the leading minority member of the committee, placed the testimony on his Web site.

One testimonial came from Mike West, who said that prior to working for Halliburton, he was employed as an area manager for Valero Energy with a yearly salary of seventy thousand dollars. "When I heard about a chance to earn more with Halliburton, I called them up," he said. "After just a few minutes, the woman said I was hired as a labor foreman at a salary of $130,000. I didn't even have to send in a resume."

When he arrived, West explained he was paid despite the fact that he had no work. "I only worked one day out of six in Kuwait," he explained. "That day, a supervisor told me to operate a forklift. I explained that I didn't have a license to operate a forklift or any experience. The response was: 'It's easy and no one will know.'"

When West got to Camp Anaconda in southern Iraq, he says that he didn't have any work to do, nor did most of the other thirty-five workers. The supervisors told them to walk around and look busy. Then they went to a camp in Al Asad, where they worked only one of every five days. They were told to bill for twelve hours of labor every day. From there, his group was sent to Fallujah for six weeks, where once again he had almost no work to do except help with security and follow Iraqi workers around to make sure they cleaned the toilets properly.

"One day, I was ordering some equipment. I asked the camp manager if it was OK to order a drill," West said.

> He said to order four. I responded that we didn't need four. He said: "Don't worry about it. It's a cost-plus contract." I asked him, "So basically, this is a blank check?" The camp manager laughed and said, "Yeah." He repeated this over and over again to the employees. As a Halliburton employee, I was disappointed by all of the company's lies and disorganization. As a taxpayer, I'm disgusted by all of the money spent by Halliburton to pay employees to do nothing.[25]

SLEEPING BAGS AND ICE

Several others described similar scams to beat the twenty-five-hundred-dollar competitive bidding clause. The Al Hasawi Industrial Group received an order for 500 sleeping bags to be delivered to a military base the same night, chopped into four separate orders for 125 sleeping bags, with each order right at the twenty-five-hundred-dollar threshold.[26]

Halliburton has also been accused of taking advantage of vague military instructions. For example, the company was given a priority order to provide troops in Kuwait and Iraq with ice in the summer. The order stated: "The contractor shall produce or subcontract and make available potable ice." So Halliburton built a plant in southern Kuwait with a

walk-in freezer and delivery dock, and imported two indus-
trial-size ice makers from east Texas that could churn out
forty tons a day. It hired twenty-eight people to run the plant
around the clock. And it stamps every bag of ice produced:
"KBR Iceworks Inc. Serving the U.S. Military."

"The deluxe ice service shows how KBR has made the
most of its unique and powerful role as the sole provider of
many support services to the military. KBR's contract with
the military contains big incentives to deliver goods and
services in a hurry to keep Army brass happy—with little
attention to the cost or efficiency of the solution," wrote
Russell Gold, a *Wall Street Journal* reporter.[27]

GHOST TRUCKS

In addition to purchasing supplies, Halliburton has also been
given the job of transporting them to the military. For these
transportation services, Halliburton billed the taxpayer $327
million by the end of spring 2004 and was expecting to get
paid another $230 million more.

But twelve current and former truckers who regularly
made the three-hundred-mile supply run from Camp Cedar
in southern Iraq to Camp Anaconda near Baghdad told a
Knight Ridder reporter that they drove as many as one in
three trucks empty.

Much of the time, drivers would drop off one empty trailer and pick up another empty one for the return trip. "There
was one time we ran 28 trucks, one trailer had one pallet (a
trailer can hold as many as 26 four-foot square pallets) and
the rest of them were empty," said David Wilson, who was
the convoy commander on more than one hundred runs. Four
other drivers who were with Wilson confirmed his account.

"It was supposed to be critical supplies that the troops had to have to operate," said Wilson, who returned to his home in southwest Florida after being fired by Halliburton. "It was one thing to risk your life to haul things the military needed. It's another to haul empty trailers."

In testimony submitted to Waxman, Wilson also described what appeared to be a complete lack of cost controls and systems to maintain equipment properly. "When I arrived at Camp Arifjan in Kuwait last November, I noticed 50 to 100 brand new trucks sitting there unused," Wilson remembered.

> Five months later, when I came home. A large number of trucks were still there, not being used. These are $85,000 (or more) Mercedes and Volvo trucks.
>
> As every other trucker working on those convoys will tell you, KBR had virtually no facilities in place to do maintenance on these trucks. There were absolutely no oil filters or fuel filters for months on end. I begged for filters but never got any. I was told that oil changes were out of the question. KBR removed all the spare tires in Kuwait. So when one of our trucks got a flat tire on the highway, we just had to leave it there for the Iraqis to loot, which is just crazy. I remember saying to myself when it happened, "You just lost yourself an $85,000 truck because of a spare tire." We lost a truck because we didn't have a $25 hydraulic line to assist the clutch.[28]

One unnamed Halliburton driver who shot videotape of the fifteen empty trailers on the road in January 2004 described it this way: "This is just a sample of the empty trailers we're hauling called 'sustainer.' And there's more behind me. There's another one right there.... This is fraud and abuse right here."

Seven of the twelve truckers who talked to *Knight Ridder* asked that they not be identified by name. Six of the twelve were fired by Halliburton for allegedly running Iraqi drivers off the road when the latter attempted to break into the convoy. The drivers disputed that accusation. In addition to interviewing the drivers, *Knight Ridder* reviewed records of the empty trips, dozens of photographs of empty flatbeds, and a videotape that showed fifteen empty trucks in one convoy.

Linda Theis, a spokeswoman for the U.S. Army Field Support Command in Rock Island, Illinois, said that military commanders and company officials might choose to run empty trucks as a security measure. The empty trailer runs in Iraq were at their highest in January, February, and March of 2004, but, as the attacks on the convoys increased exponentially, the military decided that the tactic was not working.

Halliburton officials said empty runs resulted from a lack of cargo at one depot—the company ran all the trucks so they'd be available to pick up cargo for the return trip—but drivers discounted that explanation. "Sometimes we would go with empty trailers; we would go both ways," said one driver who went by the nickname Swerve and declined to be named for fear of retribution. "We'd turn around and go back with empty trailers."[29]

FROM STOLEN TECHNOLOGY TO ROBBING THE TAXPAYER

Halliburton has a history of employing dubious tactics to profit from contracts. The company was founded in 1919 by

Earle Halliburton with patented technology stolen from Halliburton's former employer, the Perkins Oil Well Cementing Company.[30] Over the years, the company has expanded to become the world's biggest supplier of services to the oil companies, from Exxon to Shell, profiting greatly from almost every major oil-drilling scheme in the world. Some say that the profits were excessive. Indeed the company was found guilty of fixing the prices of marine construction in the oil industry over a sixteen-year period in the Gulf of Mexico, paying out over $90 million in claims and fines in the 1970s.[31] In 2002 the company admitted that one of their employees in Nigeria was caught attempting to bribe a tax inspector for $2.4 million.[32]

The construction and engineering subsidiary, Brown & Root Services, was developed in 1919 by brothers George and Herman Brown, and their brother-in-law, Dan Root. Brown & Root grew from supervising small road-paving projects to building enormously complex oil platforms, dams, and navy warships,[33] with help along the way from powerful political patrons. As Robert Caro describes in his biography of Lyndon Johnson,[34] Brown & Root had a symbiotic relationship with Johnson throughout his career and was rewarded with big government contracts—from dams in Texas, to a share in the consortium of four companies that built about 85 percent of the infrastructure needed by the army during the Vietnam War.[35] At the time, the company was heavily criticized for war-profiteering and lax controls: the General Accounting Office (GAO) reported that the company lost accounting control of $120 million and their security was so poor that millions of dollars worth of equipment had been stolen.[36]

At the time, Donald Rumsfeld, then a Republican member of the House of Representatives from Illinois, demanded to know about the "30-year association, personal and political, between Lyndon Johnson as congressman, senator, vice president and president" and the company's chairman, George R. Brown of Houston, who "had contributed $23,000 to the President's Club while the Congress was considering" whether to continue another multimillion-dollar Brown & Root project. (Club membership could be bought for $1,000 in those days.)[37]

TRICKY DICK

With the Democrats out of office, Halliburton has conveniently switched sides, so much so that the company is now being defended by the Republicans who claim that the attacks are simply an election-year smear campaign against Dick Cheney, current U.S. vice-president and former chief executive officer of the company. While it is true that the Democrats have spearheaded attacks on Halliburton during the 2004 election year, there are a few undeniable facts that back up such claims by Democrats and other Halliburton critics. Halliburton is easily the biggest contractor to the United States government in Iraq, earning three times as much as Bechtel, its nearest competitor. The company earned $3.9 billion from the military in 2003, a dizzying 680 percent increase from 2002 when it earned just $483 million.[38]

How did Halliburton get so many lucrative contracts? Friends in high places, is what most critics will tell you. Company officials will point out that very few companies have the experience to do what the company does, but this ignores the fact that the company practically designed the modern system of outsourcing the American military with the help of one man: Dick Cheney.

Cheney has worked in the Washington scene for thirty-five years. His career in the nation's capital began in 1969 as a special assistant to the director of the Office of Economic Opportunity. In 1971 he became a White House staff assistant, and soon moved on to become assistant director of the Cost of Living Council, where he stayed until 1973. After a year in private business, he returned to the White House to become deputy assistant to President Gerald Ford (1974–75) and then was appointed White House chiefs of staff (1975–77). In November 1978, Cheney, a Republican, was elected Wyoming's representative at large in the House of Representatives. For most of the eighties, Cheney served in the House of Representatives.[39]

In 1988, after the election of George Bush Sr., he was named secretary of defense. The end of the Cold War brought with it expectations of a "peace dividend" and Cheney's mandate was to reduce forces, cut weapons systems, and close military bases. Not surprisingly this was opposed by every member of Congress that depended on military pork-barrel spending to buy votes in their districts. Cheney didn't worry too much about that. He simply proposed to cut all the military spending in Democratic constituencies—notably in the districts of Thomas Downey, David Bonior, and Jim Wright, all high-profile Democrats. Jane Mayer of the *New Yorker* says that a Democratic aide on the House Armed Services Committee during those years told her that "contrary to his public image, which was as a reasonable, quiet, soft-spoken, and inclusive personality, Cheney was a rank partisan." The aide said that Cheney practiced downsizing as political jujitsu. Indeed Mayer says that her sources told her that Cheney developed a great deal of contempt for members of Congress, whom he regarded as "a bunch of annoying gnats." Meanwhile, his affinity for business deepened. "The meetings with businessmen were the ones that really got him pumped," the former aide told Mayer.[40]

By the time Cheney was done, the number of soldiers was at its lowest level since the Korean War, and Halliburton was working hard on a $3.9 million strategy for providing rapid support to twenty thousand troops in emergency situations. After reading the first study, Pentagon officials then paid Halliburton another $5 million to do a follow-up study. In August 1992, Halliburton was selected by the U.S. Army Corps of Engineers to implement the plan that it had drawn up under a contract called Logistics Civil Augmentation Program (LOGCAP). The contract was a "cost-plus-award-fee, indefinite-delivery/indefinite-quantity service" which basically meant that the federal government had an open-ended mandate and budget to send Halliburton anywhere in the world to support military operations. Although the Pentagon had often used private contractors in the past, never had they relied so heavily on a single company before. The profit margins were lower than those of private-sector jobs, but the guaranteed profit, ranging between 1 percent and 9 percent, made it a no-lose situation for the company.

In December 1992, working under this new contract, Halliburton began providing assistance to United States troops overseeing the humanitarian crisis in Somalia, putting employees on the ground within twenty-four hours of the first U.S. landing in Mogadishu. By the time Halliburton left in 1995, it had become the largest employer in the country, having contracted out most of the menial work while importing experts for more specialized needs. For this job in Somalia Halliburton was paid $109 million, but when it left the country, it simply dumped its temporary labor causing riots to break out.

A Reuters reporter in Mogadishu described the incident thus:

> A demonstration by Somali workers at the United Nations compound to protest the dismissals of local laborers by an American construction company was broken up today with clubs and tear gas. The workers who were dismissed had been employed repairing roads.... United Nations spokesman, Eugene Forson, said that 91 Somali workers were laid off (but) Somali sources had said that 500 employees had been dismissed. Mr. Forson said that after fruitless negotiations, United Nations troops rushed the workers at the United Nations compound in Mogadishu with batons and tear gas.[41]

Cheney's political fortunes at the Pentagon came to an end when George Bush Sr. lost the 1992 election to Bill Clinton. After the obligatory year outside the government-industrial complex, Cheney landed a job with his former contractor, Halliburton. (Government employees are not allowed to work for the companies they may have done business with for twelve months, but after that "cooling-off" period, they can and many do make a fortune by working as lobbyists for the very people that they once supervised.) This was no ordinary job: he was hired on as chief executive officer, despite having no experience whatsoever in corporate America. What Cheney did bring with him was a trusty Rolodex and his former chief of staff, David Gribbin, whom he appointed chief lobbyist. In the last two years at their Halliburton posts, the pair notched up $1.5 billion dollars in federal loans and insurance subsidies, compared to the paltry $100 million that the company received in the five years prior to Cheney's arrival. The federal subsidies supported Halliburton's oil services contracts in Algeria, Angola, Bangladesh, and Russia. In addition, the company garnered $2.3 billion in U.S. government contracts in that time, or almost double the $1.2 billion it earned from the government in the five years before Cheney took the reins.[42]

When the 2000 elections got underway, Cheney was asked by George Bush Jr. to suggest possible candidates for vice president—so Cheney modestly recommended himself. When Dick Cheney left Halliburton in 2000 to become George Bush's running mate, he opted not to receive his leaving payment in a lump sum, but instead have it paid to him over five years for tax reasons. Halliburton made "deferred compensation" payments to Cheney of $205,298 in 2001, $162,392 in 2002, and $178,437 in 2003, sums almost equal to his annual vice-presidential salary of $198,000.[43]

In addition, Halliburton's board voted to award him early retirement when he quit his job, even though he was too young to qualify under his contract. That flexibility enabled him to leave with a retirement package, including stock and options worth millions more than if he had simply resigned. Today he owns 433,000 stock options in the company worth over $10 million, although this total fluctuates with the value of the company's shares.[44]

A report by the Congressional Research Service, generated at the request of Senator Frank Lautenberg, a New Jersey Democrat, states that the deferred compensation that Cheney receives from Halliburton, as well as the stock options he possesses "is considered among the 'ties' retained in or 'linkages to former employers' that may 'represent a continuing financial interest' in those employers which makes them potential conflicts of interest."

This contradicts Cheney's statement made September 14, 2003, on NBC television's *Meet the Press* where he claimed, "I have no financial interest in Halliburton of any kind and haven't had, now, for over three years.... I've severed all my ties with the company, gotten rid of all my financial interest."[45]

When Cheney joined forces with Bush he took Gribbin with him, naming him director of congressional relations for the Bush-Cheney transition team, where Gribbin managed the confirmation process for newly nominated cabinet secretaries and "worked with members of Congress and state governors on issues critical to the establishment of the new administration." Subsequently, Gribbin left to head up the Prosperity Project, a political advocacy group for big business.[46]

At Halliburton, Gribbin left behind a worthy successor who became Halliburton's chief Washington lobbyist: Admiral Joe Lopez, recently retired from the U.S. Navy and former commander-in-chief of the Southern Forces Europe, also a close confidante of Dick Cheney. Lopez's first job at Halliburton, when he joined in 1999, was a $100 million contract to upgrade 150 U.S. embassy and consulate buildings around the world, to secure them against "terrorist" attacks. In March 2002, Lopez was appointed to the bipartisan Commission on Post-Conflict Reconstruction, set up by the Center for Strategic and International Studies to develop specific proposals to enhance U.S. participation in international reconstruction efforts in war-torn countries such as Afghanistan, Bosnia, and Kosovo. Other members of the commission include seven senators and representatives from the U.S. Congress, no doubt useful friends when it came to cashing in on the reconstruction proposals.[47]

WAR IN AFGHANISTAN

In 2002, suspicious that a major windfall was coming down the pike for Halliburton, I traveled to Afghanistan and Uzbekistan to find out if the company was involved in the routing of the Taliban, but turned up little—the company denied it was doing anything in the region. "Brown & Root has not deployed nor been tasked to provide support in either country," company spokesperson Zelma Branch told me in mid-April.

That same day a source in the army tipped me off. My hunch was right; I was just early. On April 26, 2002, three Halliburton employees arrived at the Khanabad air base in central Uzbekistan to begin the first civilian takeover of a United States military base in the Afghanistan "theater of operations." Within two weeks the numbers of Halliburton employees had swelled to 38, and by June 10 these men replaced the 130 military personnel that previously oversaw day-to-day support services at the two Force Provider prefabricated military bases which housed over 1,000 soldiers from the Green Berets to the Tenth Mountain Division.

New troops arriving at the base were soon being assigned sleeping quarters by the Brown & Root employees who wore khaki pants, black or blue golf shirts, and baseball caps to distinguish themselves from the soldiers. In addition, the Brown & Root employees were made responsible for laundry, food, and general base-camp maintenance as well as airfield services. Within months the company took responsibil-

ity for running the Bagram and Kandahar bases in
Afghanistan.

"Civilian contractors are meeting the Army's changing
needs. Today we are able to deploy private companies at 72
hours notice while in the past it could take 120 to 180 days
to get permission for such operations," Mike Noll, chief for
plans and operations for the LOGCAP contract who oversees
Brown & Root, explained to me in a telephone interview
from the U.S. Army Operations Support Command in
Alexandria, Virginia.[48]

By the latter part of the year, the Pentagon foresaw a
greater role for Halliburton than just maintaining operations
once state engineers had set things up. As the White House
mounted pressure on Saddam Hussein and realized their soldiers would be in short supply, the Army Corps of Engineers
contracted the company to prepare several new bases in the
Kuwaiti desert for a possible invasion of Iraq.

Army officials working with Halliburton said the collaboration helped cut costs. Compared to the cost of paying regular army salaries, Halliburton's fee for the same work
(which they would in turn subcontract out) would be just a
fraction. "We can quickly purchase building materials and
hire third-country nationals to perform the work. This
means a small number of combat-service-support soldiers
are needed to support this logistic aspect of building up an
area," said Lieutenant Colonel Rod Cutright, the senior
LOGCAP planner for all of Southwest Asia.[49]

In September 2002, Joyce Taylor of the U.S. Army Materiel
Command's Program Management Office, arrived to super-
vise approximately 1,800 Halliburton employees as they set
up tent cities that would provide accommodation for tens of
thousands of soldiers and officials. The man in charge of the

Halliburton's side of the task, coincidentally, was a man who used to do the same job in the army for thirty-two years: Robert (Butch) Gatlin, a wizened fifty-nine-year-old Tennessean. The difference this time, was that he probably earned a multiple of his army salary by taking off his camouflage battle gear and slipping into more casual civilian clothes. "When we got here, there was no power or water, I had a thousand people working here in twenty-four hours, the Army can't do that," he told a *New York Times* reporter.[50]

Within a matter of weeks, these Halliburton employees turned the rugged desert north of Kuwait City into an armed camp that would eventually support some eighty thousand foreign troops, roughly the equivalent of 10 percent of Kuwait's native-born population. Some of the encampments were named after the states associated with the attacks of September 11, 2001: Camp New York, Camp Virginia, and Camp Pennsylvania.

The headquarters for this effort was Camp Arifjan, where a gravel terrace with plastic picnic tables and chairs was surrounded by all the familiar comforts of home: in-tent Burger King, Subway, and Baskin-Robbins outlets, Pepsi machines, and a Nautilus-equipped health club with an aerobics room (featuring "Latin Dance Thurs & Sat!") greeted soldiers at the camp. Basketball hoops and volleyball nets were set up outside the mess hall.[51]

Nor was this the only locale for Halliburton's support for the invasion. North of Iraq approximately fifteen hundred Halliburton hires were stationed at the Incirlik military base near the city of Adana, about an hour's drive inland from the Mediterranean coast of central Turkey. Here they supported approximately two thousand U.S. soldiers staffing Operation Northern Watch's Air Force F-15 Strike Eagles and F-16

Fighting Falcons monitoring the no-fly zone above the thirty-sixth parallel in Iraq.[52]

Cheap labor was the primary reason for outsourcing services, said Major Toni Kemper, head of public affairs at the base. "The reason that the military goes to contracting is largely because it's more cost effective in certain areas. I mean there was a lot of studies years ago as to what services can be provided via contractor versus military personnel. Because when we go contract, we don't have to pay health care and all the another things for the employees, that's up to the employer."[53]

OCCUPIED IRAQ

In April 2003, when U.S. troops took over Iraq, Halliburton deployed engineers to help put out oil well fires and repair the dilapidated oil fields. (Saddam Hussein's troops set fire to Kuwait's oil wells after they were forced out of the country in 1991, so the army worried that he might do the same when the Americans invaded Iraq. This time their fears turned out to be overblown, as only seven wells were set on fire.) Overseeing this effort was Brigadier General Robert Crear, U.S. Army Corps of Engineers. In the days after the war he commuted twice a week to his new job from Kuwait. "It's nation-building. It's starting from scratch," he told a Texas newspaper.[54]

Dan Baum described the scene in *The New York Times Magazine*:

> The huge effort to restore Iraq's oil industry begins every day two hours south of the Iraq-Kuwait border, at the lavish Crowne Plaza Hotel in Kuwait

City. No sooner does the lobby restaurant open at 5 a.m. than a line of middle-aged men in jumpsuits, golf shirts and identical tan caps forms at the breakfast buffet, eschewing the mezzeh and labneh for French toast, home fries and beef bacon. Outside, a couple of dozen silver SUV's are lined up, and after a quick breakfast the men are off in a swift northbound convoy, each car marked with the sideways V of duct tape that designates American and British vehicles. The road knifes across a packed pebble desert as flat as a griddle, with hardly a plant or a rock gentling the view to a hazy 360-degree horizon. But nobody's minding the scenery.

The men in the SUV's are all talking at once, handing clipboards and calculators back and forth, trying to make 10,000 impossible things happen in Iraq's oil fields in exactly the right order. A couple are getting in last-minute calls to headquarters in Houston before leaving Kuwaiti cell phone coverage. Though they speak with the drawling soft consonants of the Texas-Oklahoma oil patch, these are truly citizens of the world—or at least the petroleum-producing corners of it.

For they are the legions of Kellogg Brown & Root subsidiary of the oil-services giant Halliburton, which in March won an open-ended Army contract to restore Iraq's oil fields to working order. Most have spent years toiling in the raw, scraped and sometimes violent places where oil lurks, and each hews to the oilie's ethic: no place is a hardship. How were your 12 years in Algeria? "Not bad." Your six years at Prudhoe Bay? "Not bad." Your 14 years in Nigeria? "Not bad." Southern Iraq—searing, bleak, lawless—is an assignment like any other. Also, they are very well paid.

At the border, where for most Kuwaitis formalities can take an hour, the KBR SUV's barely slow down. Each man presses his U.S. Department of Defense Contractor ID to the window, and the Kuwaiti guards wave them through. Nobody's controlling the Iraqi side. An hour later, the SUV's reach an abandoned gas station in the middle of nowhere. In the shade of crumbling walls a company of British soldiers is squatting in the sand, eating packets of weenies-and-beans from their boxed rations. They're a mixture of Royal Engineers, R.A.F. [Royal Air Force] ground troops and Seventh Armored Brigade—the famous Desert Rats who fought Rommel in North Africa. As the Brits brew tea on their folding tin stoves, Jim Koockogey, a muscular security coordinator for KBR, stands with a clipboard and shouts into the hot wind.

"Tuba Tango: we need two shooters. Arthur power station: two shooters. GOSP Three Romeo: four shooters...." From Kuwait City to here the SUV's were safe enough in their long silver convoy, but now, traveling singly, they'll need armed guards. The British soldiers toss aside the trash from their rations and drape themselves with weapons and long, glinting belts of ammunition. As the KBR cars roar off toward their daily appointments with Iraqi oil, the soldiers, many of whom fought the hard battles for Basra and Umm Qasr, pile into Land Rovers and fall in behind.[55]

This was exciting stuff for the engineers who were raking in salaries that could be as much as $120,000 a year, but less so for the Iraqi workers who feared they would soon lose their jobs. In contrast, a *Washington Post* reporter traveling in the region at about the same time as Baum, described the Iraqis thus:

The oil workers stood listlessly in front of the plant, hair blown brittle by a dusty wind, as they shared cigarettes and bitterness for lack of anything else to do. They complained about the looting that has left them without a chair to sit on, let alone a tool to wield. They worried about whether the state oil company can continue to pay them. They wondered when crude might again flow thick through their oil-gas separation plant, bound for the refinery up the road in Basra.

Then, a sparkling GMC Yukon with Kuwaiti license plates pulled up to the gate. Out stepped a round-faced American in blue jeans and a khaki baseball cap bearing the letters "KBR".... Jim Humphries breezed past the gathering with a perfunctory nod and entered the plant. Minutes later he headed back to his car, refusing a request for a report on what he saw inside. For many in the crowd, it was more than they could bear. They were already seething at the damage from the widespread looting that accompanied the end of the fighting. "You should cooperate," scolded Mohammed Mohee, an instrument technician, speaking in Arabic, as Humphries shrugged, backed away, then got in his car and drove off. "KBR just comes and

gives orders, but they don't do anything,"
Mohammed continued. "They don't give us anything to work with. This is our oil. This is our city,
our company. Our country. We want to clear away
the damage and move forward. We have no tools, no
instruments. No spare parts. They do nothing.
They just look and leave."

Five minutes later, a British desert-camouflage
military jeep and a silver sport-utility vehicle
pulled up, carrying six soldiers—some American,
some British, all holding assault rifles. Although
the crowd outside the plant numbered at least two
dozen, the soldiers headed directly for Mohammed.
Through an Arabic interpreter, they demanded his
name and asked whether he worked there. They left
after he showed them his identification card. The
crowd jeered.[56]

The oil contracts were just the tip of the iceberg. As the
U.S. consolidated control over Iraq, Halliburton was given
billions of dollars worth of new contracts that encompassed
everything from feeding soldiers, cutting their hair, washing
their clothes, and cleaning toilets, to delivering mail and
transporting prisoners of war. For six months it seemed as
though the company's revenue from Iraq could only rise into
the stratosphere.

ALLEGATIONS OF OVERCHARGING

The first hint that the company might have overstepped its
mark came as a result of the work of Henry Waxman and
John Dingell, two Democratic members of Congress who

had persisted in regularly writing letters to the Army Corps
of Engineers demanding further details about the company's
contracts, an activity the two politicians began soon after
the invasion of Iraq. In October 2003, a report from their
offices surfaced claiming that Halliburton was charging the
army $1.59 a gallon for gasoline, an outrageous sum consid-
ering the fact that the military can only resell it to Iraqis for
$0.05 a gallon (the price during Saddam's regime). Even more
startling were the actual figures that emerged in
December—the company was charging an average of $2.64 a
gallon and as much as $3.06 on occasion. By comparison, the
Defense Department's Energy Support Center (ESC) had
been doing a similar job supplying fuel at $1.32 a gallon, and
SOMO, the local oil company, was doing the same provision
for only $0.96 a gallon. The total bill to the taxpayer for 61
million gallons of fuel from Kuwait and about 179 million
gallons from Turkey, between May and late October, was
$383 million, over $100 million more than what local
providers, or even SOMO or the ESC, would have charged.

"I have never seen anything like this in my life," Phil
Verleger, a California oil economist and the president of the
consulting firm PK Verleger LLC told *The New York Times*.
"That's a monopoly premium—that's the only term to
describe it. Every logistical firm or oil subsidiary in the
United States and Europe would salivate to have that sort of
contract." Company spokeswoman Wendy Hall said that
the cost was so high because the company had more than
twenty trucks damaged or stolen, nine drivers injured, and
one driver killed when making fuel runs into Iraq.[57]

A couple of days later the *Wall Street Journal* revealed
that the Kuwaiti subcontractor supplying the fuel,
Altanmia, was not an oil transportation company but an

investment consultant, real-estate developer, and agent for
companies trading in military and nuclear, biological and
chemical equipment. The company's lead shareholder, it
was reported, was Najeeb al-Humaizi, a member of a prominent Kuwaiti family. The story started to get murkier when
the *Journal* published excerpts from a letter written by Mary
Robertson, a senior contracting officer at the Army Corps of
Engineers, in which she suggested that the U.S. embassy in
Kuwait was putting pressure on Halliburton to hire
Altanmia. "Since the U.S. government is paying for these
services, I will not succumb to the political pressures from
the [government of Kuwait] or the U.S. embassy to go
against my integrity and pay a higher price for fuel than necessary," the letter states.

The *Journal* reported that a source told it that the U.S.
ambassador to Kuwait, Richard Jones, who also served as a
deputy to Paul Bremer, asked officials at Halliburton and the
Corps of Engineers to complete a deal with Altanmia for
future gasoline imports, even if the company wouldn't lower
its rates.[58] In January 2004, Halliburton suddenly disclosed
that it had fired two employees who had taken $6 million in
kickbacks for the oil delivery contracts from an unnamed
Kuwaiti subcontractor. The company stressed that it
promptly told the Pentagon of the problem. "Halliburton
internal auditors found the irregularity, which is a violation
of our company's philosophy, policy and our code of ethics.
We found it quickly, and we immediately reported it to the
inspector general. We do not tolerate this kind of behavior
by anyone at any level in any Halliburton company," a
Halliburton spokeswoman said.

Concurrently a new ruse surfaced. A previously undis-
closed memorandum from a branch office of the Defense

Contract Audit Agency labeled Halliburton's internal system as "inadequate" for accurately estimating the cost of ongoing work in order to justify payment. The memo was sent to various army contracting officials. The Pentagon said it had to reject two huge proposed bills from the company, including one for $2.7 billion, because of myriad "deficiencies."[59] Waxman's office released another memo describing a briefing given by the General Accounting Office, the investigative arm of Congress, to investigators from the Government Reform Committee on February 13. In the briefing, the Waxman memo stated, GAO officials described a lack of sufficient government oversight of the Halliburton contract. Waxman's memo went on to cite the briefing as having reported that some of the contract monitoring was being done by military reservists with only two weeks' training.

Further, the memo reported that the GAO found that a $587 million contract had been approved in ten minutes based on six pages of documentation. Reportedly there was a single $700 million "discrepancy" between Halliburton's estimate of $2.7 billion to provide food and other logistics services to the government, and the company's own line-by-line breakdown of the estimated expenses. After the Defense Department's questioning, the company slashed its estimate for the work to $2 billion—though it never fully explained how it had reached the new figure.[60]

Halliburton says many of these problems were caused largely by the rapid expansion of its responsibilities. For instance, with little advance warning, the company was asked to feed 130,000 troops in July, nearly triple the 50,000 troops it fed in June 2003. "I don't think people appreciate the real-time nature of the work we're doing. This is not, 'Can you do this in two months?' This is, 'Can you do this

by the morning?'" Dave Lesar, chairman and chief executive
of Halliburton, told the *Wall Street Journal.*

ACCOUNTING IRREGULARITIES

But the Pentagon should have been aware of the inadequacies
of Halliburton's billing system, as they had been informed of
it on several occasions. In a March 2002 memo, Army Chief
Thomas White complained to three Pentagon undersecre-
taries "credible information on contract labor does not exist
internal to the [Army] Department." The army could not get
rid of "unnecessary, costly or unsuitable contracted work"
without full details of all the contracts, he wrote.[61]

Then on August 2, 2003 the Defense Contract Audit
Agency, published a report titled "Report on Audit of Billing
System Internal Controls" that found "significant deficien-
cies" in the billing methods of Halliburton's Kellogg Brown
& Root services unit.

The deficiencies "have adversely affected the organization's ability to record, process, summarize and report
billings." Unless the company fixed its billing system, the
auditors warned, "the result is significant over- and under-
billed costs" to the government.[62]

But unheeded government auditors are not Halliburton's
only fiscal critics. Halliburton subcontractors have also complained of the company's poor accounting methods. The *Wall
Street Journal* interviewed several Halliburton suppliers who
were not happy with how the company handles its accounts.
Ahdy Boutros, managing director of Idris National Trading
Company, called Halliburton after a bill for leased generators
wasn't paid within thirty days. He eventually got his money,
but it was five months late. Worse off was Jason Varghese,

general manager of Fitco Technical Services, a computer and electronics supply company, who was owed about $730,000, including past-due invoices as many as nine months old. "We're already neck-deep in the mud. We have to keep the relationship to get the money out," he told the reporter.[63]

In March 2004, in response to a criminal investigation launched by the Defense Criminal Investigation Service,[64] Halliburton announced it would suspend billing the government as a gesture of good faith. But concurrently the company froze payments to its subcontractors to the tune of $500 million in outstanding invoices. The biggest invoices were owed to Tamimi for $136 million, Kuwait-based La Nouvelle Trading for $76 million, and Event Source of Salt Lake City which claimed it was owed $87 million.[65]

And things haven't gotten better. In mid-May 2004, the Pentagon suspended another $159.5 million payment to Halliburton upon finding that the company submitted incomplete paperwork. The Pentagon released a statement reporting that a "Tiger Team" of investigators and auditors, appointed by Halliburton to look for possible problems, had calculated excess meal costs (overbilling) that amounted to more than 19.4 percent of the actual price charged for meals.[66]

Yet these figures might be low, as ex-Halliburton employees questioned the Tiger Team's work and found sloppy and inadequate practices. Marie de Young had worked for the military for ten years prior to working for Halliburton in Kosovo. In December 2003 she was hired to help oversee Operation Iraqi Freedom contracts in Kuwait. "I soon discovered that there was not a complete up-to-date list of all of the subcontracts . . . also, the document control department had provided incorrect lists to all of the task order managers from an inaccurate database," she said.

When the Tiger Team examined a subcontract, they just checked to make sure that all the forms were in the file.... They didn't assess the reasonableness of the price or consult with site managers. The team's sole purpose was to close as many subcontracts as possible, under the mistaken assumption that everything that was closed prior to the arrival of the government audit team would be exempt from further scrutiny. For three months, this Tiger Team occupied waterfront villas at the Hilton hotel and shuffled papers, but did nothing to effectively clean up old subcontracts.

We were instructed to pay invoices without verifying whether services were delivered. I personally told a KBR Tiger Team member not to pay an invoice that I knew was a double billing [but] the long term KBR employee told me I didn't know what I was doing.[67]

For example, de Young says that Halliburton paid the Kuwaiti subcontractor La Nouvelle one hundred dollars per bag for laundry services—four times more than they were paying elsewhere. That added up to more than $1 million per month. Another time, the company ordered 37,200 cases of soda at $1.50 a case, but was delivered only 37,200 *cans*, resulting in charges that were five times the normal wholesale cost for the drinks.

Meanwhile the auditors lived high on the hog. Halliburton housed the Tiger Team at the five-star Kempinski Hotel for ten thousand dollars per employee, per month. At the same time, soldiers were required to live in tents at a cost of $1.39 a day. The military requested that

Halliburton employees move into the tents, but they refused, de Young said.

"The Halliburton corporate culture is one of intimidation and fear," said de Young. "I had been advised by subcontract administrators who quit the company that employees get moved around when they get too close to the truth. I person ally observed and experienced this as a routine company practice. Ironically, other previous managers who tolerated bad practices were promoted to better paying jobs in Iraq or Houston or Jordan."

CONCLUSION: MERCENARIES OR MENIAL LABOR?

Military contractors such as Halliburton go to great lengths to explain that they are not mercenaries, pointing out that their workers are not issued weapons and never fight alongside soldiers. However, that is a somewhat simplistic argument, as Sam Gardiner, a retired Air Force colonel, told Jane Mayer: "It makes it too easy to go to war. When you can hire people to go to war, there's none of the grumbling and the political friction," he said, pointing out that many of the least-liked jobs (setting up tents, cleaning toilets, washing clothes, cooking food, doing guard duty) that are now being contracted out to firms like Halliburton were traditionally performed by reserve soldiers, who often complain the loudest.[68]

Then there is the argument that the private sector can save the taxpayer large sums of money, which sounds wonderful in theory but starts to look a little more suspect when whistle-blowers and auditors prove that overcharging is rife and ubiquitous. Stuart Bowen Jr., a former White House lawyer appointed in January 2004 to head up an inspector general's office for the occupation authorities, began working with other audit agencies to review the first $10 billion spent on some fifteen hundred contracts. He soon discovered that the Defense Contract Audit Agency had issued more than 187 audit reports related to nearly $7 billion in reconstruction work, finding $132.6 million in questionable costs and $307 million in unsupported costs. This evidence led the Pentagon to suspend $176.5 million in billings.[69]

Nor does the cost efficiency argument make sense if you look at the raw numbers for salaries—the average Halliburton contract employee (those from the United States at least) makes $80,000 a year while the soldier's salary range between $13,500 a year to $30,700 a year, according to salary.com.[70] In 2003, Halliburton charged U.S. taxpayers $3.9 billion for the war in Iraq. The estimates of how much its total contracts are worth range as high as an astronomical $18 billion.[71]

CHAPTER TWO

Reconstruction Racket

The giant steam turbine at the Najibiya power plant was quiet.
If the Russian engineers who built the original equipment over
thirty years ago stopped by to take a look, they might have had
a hard time recognizing the machinery. Over the years Iraqi
engineers had replaced many of the original blue parts with a
patchwork of white and gray makeshift materials.

Across the street the lights went out. Yaruub Jasim, the
general director of electricity for the southern region, a kind-
ly looking man in his sixties dressed neatly in a gray suit,
was apologetic. "Normally we have power twenty-three
hours a day but today there is a problem. We should have
done maintenance on these turbines in October, but we had
no spare parts and no money."

Jasim told me the needed parts were supposed to be supplied by Bechtel, a California-based company in charge of
repairing the power system under a contract to restore Iraq's
infrastructure.[72] (A Bechtel spokesperson said that the company was only responsible for "specifying the material
design parameters for spare parts" and it was up to occupation authorities to purchase and deliver the parts.)[73]

Just days before my visit in mid-December 2003, the United States government announced its decision to exclude from bidding on reconstruction contracts those countries that opposed the war. The political ramifications of this ban, and whether it would cover parts, suppliers, and subcontractors or not, weighed heavily on Jasim's mind.[74] "Three out of four of our power stations were built in Russia, Germany, and France. Unfortunately, Mr. Bush prevented the French, Russian, and German companies from [getting contracts in] Iraq three days ago," he said.

As I walked around the power plant, I noticed four brand-new, industrial-sized York air conditioners. "We got those air conditioners two weeks ago—Bechtel sent them to us because our equipment was malfunctioning over the summer, but they haven't installed them and we don't need them in the winter," said Hamad Salem, the plant's manager. The delay was due to a dispute over whether Bechtel or the power plant itself was responsible for installing the air conditioners.

The engineers in southern Iraq were lucky to have to explain why the power failed only once a day. Their colleague in Baghdad, Mohsen Hassan, the technical director for power generation at the Ministry of Electricity, had to explain to visitors why in the capital, which houses a quarter of Iraq's population, there is frequently no power for over ten hours a day.

A quiet, unassuming man, Hassan wore a checkered shirt, no tie, and a brown jacket, garb that might have been seen on any man on any street in this city. "Bechtel has put us in a very difficult position. My minister has said to them if the people get angry, don't blame us. You know electricity is the first (biggest) problem in Iraq, they must solve this as soon as possible. Under Saddam we fixed everything quick-

ly, but we didn't worry about quality. We didn't work the
standard way, it was very irregular."

One of the reasons that Bechtel took so long was because
its electrical team spent two months simply examining
power plants, substations, and high-voltage lines before they
started any work, infuriating the Iraqi staff who said they
could have told the company what was necessary. Theft and
sabotage were other problems. As soon as Bechtel started
replacing ten sabotaged electrical towers near Nassiriya,
another ten were destroyed nearby.[75]

Bechtel denied responsibility for the situation. "A lot of
people thought the United States was going to come in with
a dump truck of money," Cliff Mumm, head of Bechtel's Iraq
effort, told the *San Francisco Chronicle*. "To just walk in
and start fixing Iraq—that's an unrealistic expectation."[76]

WHO IS BECHTEL?

Bechtel won the contract from the United States Agency for
International Development (USAID) before President Bush
declared an end to major conflict in April 2003. This contract was expanded and then a second contract awarded in
January 2004, under which the company was to repair and
refurbish sewage, water, and school systems for $2.8 billion,
making Bechtel's business in Iraq second only to
Halliburton's.[77]

A month prior to the awarding of the contract, Riley
Bechtel, the multibillionaire CEO leading the family
dynasty, was sworn in as a member of President Bush's
Export Council to advise the government on creating markets for American companies overseas.[78]

The family-owned Bechtel Corporation is one of the

world's largest engineering-construction firms, with projects ranging from laying the first major oil pipelines in Alaska and Saudi Arabia, to building nuclear reactors in Qinshan, China, and running refineries in Zambia. Founded in 1898, the company has worked on 20,000 projects in 140 nations on all seven continents. In 2002, Bechtel earned $11.6 billion in revenue.[79] Buoyed in part by the Iraq contract, Bechtel reported record revenues in 2003, reversing a three-year slide. After hitting $15.1 billion in 1999, the company's previous record, revenue fell to $11.6 billion in 2002, before bouncing back to $16.3 billion for 2003.[80]

Soon after Riley Bechtel was appointed an advisor to Bush, on April 21, 2003, Terry Valenzano, the man who ran Bechtel's construction business in Saudi Arabia, flew into Kuwait City to meet with Jay Garner, the Pentagon official appointed to oversee Iraq whom Paul Bremer succeeded. The two men met at the Hilton resort and the Sheraton to plan the reconstruction of Iraq after the fall of Saddam Hussein's government.[81]

It was like a dream come true for the former secretary of state and ex–Bechtel president, George Schultz, who had penned a *Washington Post* op-ed in September 2002 urging the administration to back an attack: "A strong foundation exists for immediate military action against Hussein and for a multilateral effort to rebuild Iraq after he is gone."[82]

Indeed, for him, it was just like old times. Twenty years ago, on December 20, 1983, Middle East peace envoy Donald Rumsfeld arrived in Baghdad on a special mission from George Shultz (then secretary of state for President Ronald Reagan) to meet with Saddam Hussein. Rumsfeld asked the Iraqi dictator to support Bechtel's bid on construction of an oil pipeline from Iraq to the Jordanian port of Aqaba.[83]

That's not all. Jack Sheehan, a senior vice president at

Bechtel, is a member of the Defense Policy Board, a government-appointed group that advised the Pentagon on the war. Meanwhile Bechtel also advises both the federal agencies that provide loans and insurance to American companies overseas. Daniel Chao, another Bechtel senior vice president, serves on the advisory board of the U.S. Export Import Bank (ExIm), while Ross Connelly, a twenty-one-year veteran of Bechtel, is the chief operating officer for the Overseas Private Investment Corporation (OPIC).[84]

Indeed, Andrew Natsios, the administrator of USAID, which awarded the reconstruction contract for Iraq, was overseeing Bechtel just two years prior, as the chairman of the Massachusetts Turnpike Authority, which hired the company to complete the Boston Central Artery project.[85]

Watchdog groups predicted that the incestuous relationship between Bechtel and the U.S. government would bode ill for the Iraqi people. "Bechtel and privatization go hand in hand. As people learned the hard way in Bolivia and around the world, when Bechtel comes to town, you can expect costs to soar and accountability and local control to evaporate," said Juliette Beck, senior organizer at Public Citizen's California office.[86] Bechtel had recently brought a $25 million lawsuit against Bolivia for canceling a contract to manage the Cochabamba water system. Under Bechtel, the water rates for locals skyrocketed.[87]

Boston taxpayers have been just as unlucky. The Boston Central Artery tunnel project (popularly known as the "Big Dig") is wrapping up the reconstruction of Interstate 93 underneath the surface of the city. In 1985, the price tag of the project was an estimated $2.5 billion. This figure has been spiraling upwards every year. The latest price tag for the project was a whopping $14.6 billion or $1.8 billion a mile, making it the world's most expensive high-way.[88]

And California citizens are still paying the bills for the cost overruns at the San Onofre nuclear power plant in northern San Diego County where Bechtel installed one of the reactors backwards. Meanwhile, the local environmental costs continue to mount every day as the plant sucks in huge quantities of plankton, fish, and even seals with the water needed to cool the reactors. The reactor also destroys tons of kelp on the seabed by discharging the heated water back into the ocean.[89]

Other construction boondoggles by Bechtel include the Ok Tedi gold mine in Papua New Guinea where in 1984 the dam Bechtel was building to contain mining waste collapsed before gold was ever extracted. In 1996, when the local people took them to court, BHP, the Australian operators of the mine, agreed to spend up to $115 million to contain the toxic waste that they were dumping into the Fly River at a rate of eighty thousand tons a day.[90]

The Bechtel Group and its employees have also been among the biggest political donors in the construction industry, according to an analysis by the Center for Responsive Politics, a nonpartisan, Washington-based group that tracks campaign finances.[91]

The center found that the company and its workers contributed at least $277,050 to federal candidates and party committees in the last election cycle: about 57 percent to Democrats and 43 percent to Republicans. Center figures show that Bechtel gave at least $166,000 to national Republican Party committees.

GOOD NEWS GUYS

To its credit, Bechtel is one of the few companies that does make extensive use of local contractors and holds regular meetings to explain how to get work from them. It is also the most accessible to the international press, being the only company to maintain offices at the Baghdad Convention Center, where the U.S. military held trainings, meetings, and press conferences for the outside world. However, the company was not as accessible to ordinary Iraqis. Getting to Bechtel's offices wasn't easy. It took half an hour on a good day to get through the obstacle course designed to keep out suicide bombers, comprising three body searches and a maze of barbed wire, sandbags, solid concrete road blocks, and soldiers.

In December 2003, on a visit to Bechtel and USAID offices in the heavily guarded Baghdad Convention Center next to the Republican Palace, I encountered three heavily armed men with assault rifles in the central atrium. They walked in step, facing different directions, scanning the area constantly. In the center of the circle they created was an older man in a blazer. He looked like a career politician, and he was smiling as he chatted with the woman walking beside him.

"This looks so splendid," he proclaimed, gesturing at the convention center. I asked the armed men who he was, perhaps a member of Congress? "No, he's Ambassador Ted Morris, who runs Baghdad and its suburbs." So I stepped up and asked him if he would speak to me for a few minutes about the infrastructure problems in the city. He smiled genially. "Of course."

Morris focused entirely on the positive. "When we came here, the entire city was still without light. The entire city was insecure and there was fighting going on. But now, in terms of the whole city, there has been tremendous, tremendous progress."

When I told him that I had talked with the power plant managers and they had a different story to tell, he assured me that everything would be resolved in time. He insisted

Six months is a little unrealistic to ask for [the reconstruction] to be over. The bottleneck is sheer time. If you look at how much time it took to rebuild [in] Bosnia, in Sierra Leone, in Rwanda, in Cambodia, in Burundi, in Timor. Wherever you have had a true conflict situation, there is an impatience in that people think it could be done immediately. Never in the world can it be done immediately. It cannot. It's just a physical engineering constraint and it has nothing to do with Bechtel.[92]

Mohsen Hassan didn't agree. "We, the Iraqi engineers, can repair anything," he said. "But we need money and spare parts, and so far Bechtel has provided us with neither. The only thing that the company has given us so far is promises. We have brought the power generation up to four hundred megawatts without any spare parts, but we will need something more than words if we want to provide this city with the twenty-eight hundred megawatts that it demands."

Of course certain infrastructure repair projects did get more than empty promises—the dredging of the Umm Qasr seaport and the Baghdad airport got top priority. These projects were quickly executed because the military needed to bring in equipment for the occupation. And within weeks in the spring of 2003, mobile phone towers had sprung up to provide MCI service to American officials and their appointed Iraqi advisors.

UMM QASR

One of the only infrastructure projects to be completed on time was the port of Umm Qasr, on the Persian Gulf's northwestern tip. Put simply, the site was essential to bring in heavy equipment and other supplies to support the occupation. Within four months the port was dredged by Great Lakes Dredging Company of Illinois, under subcontract to Bechtel, and then turned over to Stevedoring Services of America (SSA), a company that runs many of the major Pacific ports in the United States.

Built in 1958 by Iraqi nationalists, the Umm Qasr port was the crown jewel of the export trade. From its piers, Iraq began to ship goods from Iraqi factories to buyers in other countries throughout the region. The port became a symbol of progress and independence, an achievement of the Iraqi revolution.[93] But almost fifty years later, the narrow channel hadn't been dredged in a decade, so large cargo ships couldn't approach. Other dangers included unexploded weapons from past wars and the hulks of perhaps a half-dozen wrecked ships.

Great Lakes brought in a self-propelled cutter-suction dredger called Aquarius that dug and sucked 4.4 million cubic yards of muck from the channel floor over the first four months, dumping it on an empty stretch of sand across from the dock. Small ships armed with towering cranes heaved wrecks, or pieces of them, out of the water. Divers probed the channel floor for metal objects that could be old bombs or missiles, identifying the weapons by careful touch.

Bechtel supervisor Patrick Larkin showed David Baker, a *San Francisco Chronicle* reporter, around the dredging operations at the port in late summer 2003. Baker wrote: "A ship's rusting frame hung over the dock at Umm Qasr in mid-August, dripping seawater and silt. Metal cables thick as phone poles had just pulled the wreck from the channel floor and now held it suspended in air, slicing the aging hull like a wire through cheese."[94]

In parallel to the dredging operation, USAID brought in SSA Marine, a $1 billion-a-year, family-owned business from Seattle, Washington, to manage the port. Labor activist David Bacon told CorpWatch that SSA had a long history of antilabor policies, which they exported to Iraq. Their close ties to the Bush administration were revealed in 2002, during the labor negotiations between the Pacific Maritime Association (PMA), an employers association of which SSA was the most virulently antiunion member, and the International Longshore and Warehouse Union (ILWU).

> Weeks before the contract expired on July 31, the administration began to intervene directly. Homeland Secretary Tom Ridge, and then Labor Secretary Elaine Chao, both told the union's bargaining committee that the administration would prevent any strike. They made clear that Bush would begin by invoking the Taft-Hartley Act, under which striking longshoremen would be prevented from stopping work for eighty days. In addition, they said, the union's coastwise bargaining

structure might be declared an illegal monopoly, meaning that if the union struck one port, shippers could simply load and unload their cargo in another, making strikes pointless.

Finally, the Bush officials said, the government would replace striking longshoremen with Navy personnel in the huge cargo cranes that load and offload the giant shipping containers. All the Bush proposals had the same immediate intent—removing the union's bargaining leverage by making a waterfront strike impossible.

When the ILWU avoided being provoked into a strike, the PMA locked workers out of the terminals in late September 2002. The employers then demanded Bush invoke the Taft-Hartley Act, and after ten days, got what they wanted. Despite the fact that they themselves had closed the gates of their own terminals, the Bush administration got a federal judge to order the union to work under its old contract, with no interruption, for eighty days.[95]

Back in Iraq, despite the Workers Democratic Trade Union Federation's June 2003 efforts to set up an organization for dockers and other transport workers, there was still no union on the docks in Umm Qasr by the end of 2003, according to one retired longshore union organizer, Muhsen Mull Ali. "In Basra 70 percent of the people are unemployed," Mull Ali told Bacon. "American companies hire Iraqis at $70, and foreigners at $300. There's so much unemployment in Iraq that people will take jobs at any wage, and the Americans took advantage of this."

Mull Ali spent two long stints in prison for organizing

unions in Basra (first under the king, and then under
Saddam), but said he intended to return to the area neverthe-
less to begin reorganizing workers on the docks, "They will
reimpose capitalism on us, so our responsibility is to oppose
privatization as much as possible, and fight for the welfare
of our workers."[96]

To make matters worse, complaints have started to trick-
le in from the customers themselves about the blatant profiteering at the port. Behnam Polis, the Iraqi minister of
transportation, told *Newsweek* that SSA was overcharging.
"They're unloading cargo at $12 a ton. That's a lot. Ports in
Dubai and Kuwait do it for $3 a ton," he said. "A lot of ships
are not coming because it costs too much." Polis chalked
the problem up to the United States' guarantee to pay the
company no matter how much work it did. That's nonsense,
SSA spokesman Bob Waters told *Newsweek*, explaining that
SSA originally set high cargo tariffs to make the port "self-
sustaining." Later he claimed Polis's own ministry took control and didn't change the prices.[97]

WAITING AND SEETHING

Inland, Iraqs waited for basic repairs. And waited. And waited. By the end of the first six months of occupation, which
unfortunately coincided with the worst of the summer heat,
local people were ready to riot. Mohammad Kasim Hamady,
a Basra citizen told the *San Francisco Chronicle*, "If they
think we're used to this, they're wrong. We're decent people.
We have the right to a civilized life." He said he was tired of
sleeping on the roof, of enduring the rashes that Basra's 125-
degree air erupts on his skin, of seeing his children wander
listless through the house in their underwear when the

blackouts hit. "We didn't ask them to come. We need all the basic needs. If they don't like that, they can go home."

A year after occupation, as local people reached their wits' end, the question of whether Bechtel could have repaired the infrastructure more quickly was almost moot. Iraqis pointed out that the previous regime got things up and running again after the first Gulf War in a matter of months, despite the fact that the damage was much more extensive because the United States and Britain strategically bombed the power infrastructure.

Bechtel, on the other hand, clings to its claims that although the power plants were not bombed in the 2003 invasion, ten years of sanctions and neglect have taken their toll, making repairs much more difficult and time consuming than they were in 1991. However, the scale of the task should have come as no surprise to Bechtel or the administration, which critics suggest should have been better prepared.

Indeed a report by the New York–based Global Policy Forum in August 2001 stated:

> Civilian infrastructure has suffered disproportionately from the lack of maintenance and investment. For example, Iraq's electrical sector is barely holding production steady at one-third of its 1990 capacity even though government expenditure in the sector consistently exceeds plans. Electrical shortages, worst during the hot summers, spoil food and medicine and stop water purification, sewage treatment, and irrigated agriculture, interfering with all aspects of life.[98]

Regardless, Iraqi engineers maintain they could fix things right away were they only given the chance. "The Americans have very high standards, ours are very low," said Mohsen Hassan from the ministry, holding out his hands and bringing them closer together to illustrate his point. "We need to meet in between." I asked him why Bechtel is so slow in Iraq, given their competence building the Saudi Arabian electricity system from scratch. "These are unusual circumstances," says Hassan. "No security, there is sabotage, the system is upset."[99]

Yet the complaints are not limited to electricity. Most telephones didn't work for a long time after the invasion—some were still not working when I last visited in April 2004—because of the precision bombing of phone exchanges by U.S. and British planes. Bechtel engineers struggled for over a year to get them working again, but regular sabotage ensured that this continued to be a work in progress.

WHITEWASHING SCHOOLS

The situation in Iraq's schools, which Bechtel was supposed to have repaired over the summer of 2003, was not much better. An internal study by U.S. Army personnel surveying Iraqi Education Ministry staff and school principals was leaked to *Cox Newspapers* in late 2003. The report strongly criticized Bechtel's attempts to renovate Iraqi schools.

"The new fans are cheap and burned out immediately upon use. All inspected were already broken," wrote one U.S. soldier. "Lousy paint job. Major clean-up work required. Bathrooms in poor condition," wrote another about a different school.

Much of the criticism focused on Bechtel's Iraqi subcon-

tractors. "The contractor has demanded the schools' managers to hand over the good and broken furniture. The names
of the subcontractors are unknown to us because they did
not come to our office," wrote an Iraqi school planner.

"In almost every case, the paint jobs were done in a
hurry, causing more damage to the appearance of the school
than . . . providing a finish that will protect the structure.
In one case, the paint job actually damaged critical lab
equipment, making it unusable."[100]

Bechtel officials defended their work. "The people at
Bechtel really care about this one. We've all got kids. We've
all been to school. In a country with a lot of hurt, this is
meaningful. So, it's a system, it's people who care and it's
being done in the middle of chaos, chaos evolving into some
thing more orderly and more Iraqi," Bechtel's Gregory
Huger, a manager in the reconstruction program, told the
Cox reporter.

But Cox was not the only media organization to write
about the Iraqi school scandal. Newsweek reporters say they
visited five schools in Baghdad's Camp Sara neighborhood,
all of which were among those listed as rebuilt by different
Iraqi contractors working for Bechtel. None had enough
textbooks, desks, or blackboards. Most schools were strewn
with refuse everywhere, had toilets that didn't properly
work, and housed two-seater desks made to accommodate
four. Ahmed Majid Jassim, a pro-U.S. headmaster told the
reporter, "Americans have made a great effort. I've seen
rebuilt schools, and this isn't one of them."[101]

And Karim El-Gawhary, an Egyptian reporter for the well-
known Cairo-based weekly Al Ahram heard similar complaints as he toured several schools. Dr. Nabil Khudair
Abbas, from the planning center at the Ministry of

Education, which is responsible for a quarter of Baghdad's schools, told El-Gawhary that he had been meeting with Bechtel representatives on a weekly basis and presenting his complaints. He said that the program was anything but transparent, and none of the work was being checked. Nobody in the Ministry of Education knew exactly how much money the United States had paid Bechtel to implement the program, nor the details of the work to be carried out in individual schools.[102]

In Baghdad, I visited four schools, beginning with Al-Harthia, a low, white building which houses 570 elementary school students. Here I met Huda Sabah Abdurasiq, who lost no time in showing me all that was wrong: rain leaked through the ceiling, shorting out the power; the new paint was already peeling; and the floor had not been completely repaired.

Most shocking to Abdurasiq was the price tag. "I could fix everything here for just one thousand dollars. Mr. Jeff [a Bechtel subcontractor] spent twenty thousand!" she fumed. She went to the district council and complained and then marched off to the convention center to confront the military. "They were very angry and spoke to our councilmember Hassan but nothing happened. And we have no receipts for money spent. It's useless, they won't do a thing," she said.

I headed over to Al-Wathba school, which was easily in the worst condition of all the schools I visited. Ahmad Abdu-Satar, a friendly man who had worked there for two years, showed me the toilets and sinks. The faucets were fitted with new brass taps and the doors painted a dark blue, but the sinks were in a terrible state. They looked like they hadn't been touched in a decade. The walls needed painting and, like the previous school, the playground was flooded.

"I've been thinking of turning it into a swimming pool," he remarked sarcastically. "Honestly, nothing has changed since Saddam's time. I ask you, would American children use these toilets?" I told him that budgets have been slashed in America and teachers fired en masse, but he repeated his question: "I ask you, would American children use these toilets?"

"We have no books, no stationary, nothing. At least we had that in Saddam's time. Yes, our salaries have gone up, but so have prices. When I asked the contractor why they didn't finish the job, they said, 'We don't work for you, we work for the Americans.'"

I stopped briefly at the Al Raja'a school, but it was still being repaired. Jamal Salih, the guard, showed me around, and then complained that he had asked the contractor to fix his house, but they refused. I took a peek inside, surprising his two daughters and wife who were busy preparing a meal of potato chips for lunch. The workers also invited me to join them for their falafel lunch, but I declined and hastened to the last stop of the day before the school day ended at 1 P.M.

The Hawa school was run by Batool Mahdi Hussain, a tall woman, dressed all in brown, including her traditional Islamic headscarf. She appeared young for the eleven years she had spent at the school, which she took over after the occupation when the parents voted her in as headmistress. Like the two previous headmistresses, she was eager to talk and show me around. She, too, was bitter about the contractors. The school had a fresh coat of paint on the outside with all of the characters from the Disney version of Aladdin, complete with the genie and the prince. But, she said, things are now worse than under Saddam. "UNICEF painted our walls and gave us new Japanese fans. They painted the cartoons outside. When the American contractors came, they took away our Japanese fans and replaced them with Syrian fans that don't work," she said angrily.

We were joined by the school guard, Ali Sekran, who spoke a few words of English. He repeatedly used his AK-47 as a pointer to help Hussain illustrate all the problems. I prayed that the gun wasn't loaded.

The headmistress took me to the toilets, where a new water system had been installed—pipes, taps, and a motor to pump the water. The problem was the motor didn't work so the toilets reeked with unflushed sewage. She then removed a new drain cover to reveal the absence of a drain underneath. She walked quickly, not waiting for the camera to catch up, a whirlwind of show-and-tell. "These doors, the hinges are broken. We were supposed to get steel doors; we got wooden doors. The new paint is peeling off. There isn't enough power to run our school," she said. I noticed a brand new chalkboard. Hussain told me that the teachers paid for it out of their own pocket. As I bade her farewell, she walked me past the gate and pointed to the construction debris in the road. "They didn't even take their rubbish with them. They gave us no papers to tell us what they had done and what they did not do. We had to pay to haul the trash. Honestly, the condition of our school was better before the contractors came."

Bechtel Baghdad spokesman Francis Canavan told me the company had "received inquiries" about a number of the schools it was contracted to repair. He said Bechtel had directed its subcontractors to make repairs, and was withholding 10 percent of the subcontractors' payment to ensure that repairs would be made. When asked whether the poor workmanship was an unusual experience for Bechtel in similar projects, Canavan pointed out that the company had

never fixed schools before. "We were hired because we are
the only people who can coordinate such a big project in a
short period of time," he told me.

But USAID was unapologetic about the state of the
schools. An official spokesperson told me "If you are going to
do a slam article that complains that the paint is peeling on a
school that we didn't fix, I don't see why I should talk to you
I don't even know that you went to schools that were fixed by
AID—twenty-six of the fifty-two schools that have submitted
complaints were not even part of our contract." I assured her
that I only visited schools that were listed by Bechtel, showing her the company's own list. She acknowledged the list
with bad grace, clearly rattled by numerous news reports on
the failure of a school repair program that officials had hoped
would bring them much-needed positive publicity.

Canavan, in a later email response from Baghdad, told me
he couldn't find the schools I visited on Bechtel's list. He
noted, however, that "school names change, and the English
spelling of school names in Iraq varies." I agreed to investigate together with him, but, on my second visit to Iraq, I ran
into another problem: the translator who had taken me to
the schools had fled Baghdad for security reasons.

Canavan and his San Francisco counterpart, Jonathan
Marshall, told me that they would declare a mistrial on the
matter of the schools I inspected. "We did find twenty-eight
schools that had problems so I won't say that we were perfect. But we expected that there would be problems and we
planned to check them after the job was done," Marshall
told me in a telephone interview in May 2004. I pointed out
that unless they had a paper trail to prove that they were
planning the audit, it looks like they acted after the fact. In
any case, this episode suggests another problem that

appeared to plague the Iraq reconstruction business and contributed to numerous disputes and delays; that is, frequent
confusion among Iraqis, occupation authorities, and contractors over who's responsible for what.[103]

WATER, WATER, EVERYWHERE,
BUT NOT A DROP TO DRINK

In May 2004, over one year after the occupation began,
Baghdad's Kerkh sewage treatment plant, which was
designed to handle the waste of more than two million people, was still not working. Instead the green-brown waste
flowed straight to the Tigris nearby. All the way to Basra, in
the towns and cities downstream residents drink from the
river, while many people swim and fish in it.

Sa'ad Mohammed, the director general of Baghdad's water
department, told me in mid-December 2003 that, "from the
beginning, the U.S. considered Iraq like Afghanistan—without infrastructure and expertise. But when they came here,
they realized the Iraqis are very different. The biggest problem is that the money allocated for water and sewage from
the $18 billion U.S. budget was not enough."[104]

In April 2004, Canavan admitted that the sewage system
had not yet been fixed, but he had an explanation: "Under
Saddam, the sewage treatment plants just dumped the waste
in the river. We can't fix it overnight," he said. But Wada,
my translator, was furious when I recounted the story to
him. "Dumped the waste in the river! Well, who bombed the
sewage plant in the first Gulf war? And who blocked the sale
of chlorine disinfectant to the treatment plants, claiming
they could be used for WMDs?"[105]

Weeks earlier, Public Citizen, a U.S. nonprofit group, called for an investigation into why Bechtel had not fulfilled the duties spelled out for the first year of its contract. "U.S. taxpayers are funding Bechtel's reconstruction contract without a means to demand accountability," said Wenonah Hauter, director of Public Citizen's Water for All campaign. "It is clear that Bechtel's lucrative contract is not helping the people of Iraq gain access to the water they desperately need to survive. The U.S. government should not subsidize profit-driven corporations that care more about dollars earned than the people served. Water is an essential commodity, not an option."[106]

Public Citizen said that one of Bechtel's earliest priorities was to ensure the provision of potable water supplies to the population of southern Iraq in the first sixty days of the program. However, one year later, the monitors say that there was little evidence that this mandate has been achieved. Rising incidents of cholera, kidney stones, and diarrhea—all waterborne illnesses—point to the failure of Bechtel's mission.

Public Citizen cited the example of the city of Hilla, whose water treatment plant and distribution center Bechtel had specifically named in its assessment report as requiring rehabilitation within six months to meet urgent needs for water. On October 17, 2003 the six-month period ended. The plant in Hilla was managed by Chief Engineer Salmam Hassan Kadel, who said that even during the war there was running water in every house. At that time the plant engineers simply needed to replace old pipes and pumps. But in the war's aftermath, looting and a lack of electricity caused the water infrastructure to fail. Despite help from UNICEF, Red Cross, and several nonprofits, the plant was only supplying 50 percent of the needed water to the people of Hilla.

By spring 2004 the surrounding villages had no water, nor had they been supplied with the pipes they needed to get the

work done. Kadel reported that his plant has had no contact
with Bechtel, or any of its subcontractors, despite complaints of massive outbreaks of cholera, diarrhea, nausea,
and kidney stones in his area.

Bechtel was acting irresponsibly by "spending all of their
money without any studies," Kadel told *Public Citizen*.

> We give our NGO's all of our information before
> they do the work, and they know what to do.
> Bechtel is painting buildings, but this doesn't give
> clean water to the people who have died [sic] from
> drinking contaminated water. We ask of them that
> instead of painting buildings, they give us one water
> pump and we'll use it to give water service to more
> people. We have had no change since the Americans
> came here. We know Bechtel is wasting money, but
> we can't prove it.[107]

When I asked Canavan about it, he dismissed the charges:

> There's a fundamental misunderstanding of what
> we are doing. Their description of the original
> USAID contract is accurate but it was also a shop-
> ping list for everything they wanted done. We did
> an assessment and told them what could be fixed
> for $680 million in the time allotted. It would take
> $16 billion to complete everything they wanted
> done. The contract also mentions 100 bridges but
> we are only working on a few. And we haven't fin-
> ished fixing the water treatment plants, and no, we
> aren't doing distribution, so of course the water
> supply is still contaminated.[108]

CREATIVE CONTRACTING

While Bechtel was put in charge of the school infrastructure and sanitation, Creative Associates International, a Washington, D.C.–based contractor was given up to $157 million by USAID to overhaul Iraq's educational system.[109] This consulting group was well known to the AID staffers because several of their former colleagues had gone to work at Creative, such as Frank Dall, a former USAID education director for the Middle East. Dall had previously worked as a senior education adviser to the United Nations Children's Fund in Jordan and was responsible for nationally based UNICEF educational programs in the Middle East.

Several months before the war, Dall took part in a round-table discussion with USAID officials about Iraq's education system. Suspicious that this roundtable discussion might have given him the inside track, Bruce Crandlemire, assistant inspector general for audit at USAID, recommended the contract be reviewed.

A June 2003 USAID memorandum detailing the findings stated, "The documentation is clear that only one of the five contractors that were subsequently invited by USAID to bid on the contract participated in an initial roundtable discussion. In addition, we conclude that USAID Bureau officials did not adhere to the guidance on practical steps to avoid organizational conflicts of interest." USAID officials apparently told the inspector general's office that they did not need to conduct "market research" required by acquisition rules because officials already knew enough to determine which companies to pick, according to the memo.[110]

Mind you, Creative Associates has a history of helping Washington selectively educate U.S. sympathizers in conflict zones. The consulting firm received USAID and

Pentagon funding to help demobilize and provide civilian training for the Contras, anticommunist guerrillas in Nicaragua who had fought the Sandinistas. In 1989, as part of a $27 million USAID package, Creative received $1 million to train Contra rebels in skills such as road maintenance, first aid, and engine repair.[111]

Creative won similar contracts resulting from the "war on terrorism," despite the availability of other more experienced contractors. For example, in Afghanistan it outbid the University of Nebraska, Omaha's (UNO) Center for Afghanistan Studies, which had been working for USAID on Afghan education for more than a decade. UNO's Center for Afghanistan Studies printed 14.2 million textbooks and trained 2,740 teachers for the 2002–03 school years.

Raheem Yaseer, assistant director of the center, said he was surprised when Creative won the 2003-04 Afghan education contract. "Our university has been involved in Afghanistan from the early 1970s, and had offices and programs during the war years," Yaseer said. "But I think last year, AID decided to put in some new blood, and people who had experience before were not given the grants," he told the Center for Public Integrity.

With its contract secure, Creative didn't bother supporting the local economy. Instead it subcontracted the printing of the Afghan textbooks to an Indonesian company, and then airlifted the books to Afghanistan.

I'M SORRY, YOUR BABY'S DEAD

The situation in the health sector is not much better, despite the millions spent on private contractors to reorganize the nation's hospitals. At the Yarmouk hospital in Baghdad, I visited the neonatal unit where I found just four scrawny babies breathing almost imperceptibly behind the plastic walls of their incubators in the half-dark ward. Pushed against the other wall were half a dozen more incubators, some donated by the United Arab Emirates, some by the United States; others were stacked in the corridor outside. All of them worked, but there was no room for them, and the hospital lacked the power and clean water required to keep them going.

Dr. Tala al Awqati reeled off statistics in a matter-of-fact manner without passion or anger. She had done the same for dozens of journalists, activists, and members of Congress but no help ever arrived. "Last year, twenty babies died out of eighty admitted, now twenty out of every fifty die. In almost every way, things are worse than before the war," she said. She has run this neonatal ward for four years, been in the business for almost seventeen years.

My trip was prompted by two articles published in early 2004—one in the London *Independent* and the other in *The New York Times*—both of which cited conditions in this hospital and the Al Iskan hospital to suggest that the occupation had caused the health situation to deteriorate dramatically.[112]

As it turned out the story was not quite as dire as the journalists suggested. Yes, deaths were up at this ward, but only because they had closed half the hospital to rehabilitate it. The staff expects that conditions will dramatically improve once the old wards are put back into service.

Bereft parents were forced to watch their newborns die because the Ministry of Health had not figured out how to repair the building and provide services at the same time. Will things be fine once the building is repaired? "Well, we still don't have much of the equipment or spare parts we need to run the incubators. We don't have the proper training and we still lack medicines," said al Awqati.

She also pointed to another undocumented problem. Admissions at the hospital had dropped because more and more women are having children at home, rather than risk the perilous trip through potential military action and traffic jams. "Spontaneous abortions have increased, many women are losing their babies before they get to hospital," she told us.

Dr. Haqqi I Razzaouki, the newly appointed general director of the hospital, was far more upbeat. "We've been accepting casualties for thirty years, we've seen four wars. The Americans bombed it in the first Gulf war, then they occupied it with tanks for two months in the war last year. This has been a battleground but now it is much, much better than a year before," he said enthusiastically.

How long had he worked there? Two weeks, he said cheerfully. "Our staff is doing their job very nicely but we have to serve half of Baghdad. Step by step we will fix everything but it will take time."[113]

But premature infants can't survive the wait. In late 2003, at the Al Iskan Central Teaching Hospital for Children (where there are more incubators and more space but the death rates haven't improved much), Dr. Hafiz Hussein was signing the death certificate for a newborn who had just died in his arms when the baby's relatives stormed into the emergency room. He said the men grabbed him and hit him in the face about twenty times. "I felt such shame. The child died and I got beaten in front of my colleagues for it."[114]

In June 2003, Andrew Natsios, head of USAID, set an objective of cutting the infant mortality rate of Iraqi babies by 50 percent.[115] Almost ten months later, Ammar al Saffar, the deputy health minister, told me that the statistics hadn't changed—they were about the same as when the occupation started.[116]

IS ABT APT FOR IRAQ'S HOSPITALS?

"I've been all around the country and we're better than pre-war levels across the board," Bob Goodwin, an American health adviser for the Coalition Provisional Authority who had been working with the Iraqi Health Ministry since summer 2003, told *The New York Times*. Many hospitals had new generators and new wiring, he said and the distribution of medical supplies was fairer now than it was under Saddam. "When we took over in April, it was a total system collapse. The health ministry was literally on fire."[117]

A year later, the ministry building in Baghdad was doing just fine—the multistoried building has been repainted and every office had nice new gray desks and filing cabinets, while the hospitals were waiting for volunteers to repair them. Bechtel did minor repair work to about fifty primary healthcare centers around the country and left the rest to USAID to take care of.

USAID spent almost a year trying to figure out who would rebuild the health care centers and hospitals. In March 2004, a small $27.7 million contract was finally awarded to a joint venture of the Louis Berger Group of New Jersey and URS corporation of San Francisco, a company partially owned by Senator Dianne Feinstein's husband, Richard Blum. Although Feinstein is one of the leading Democrats on Capitol Hill, URS had also donated more than $10,700 to President Bush's re-election campaign.[118] A month later, when I was at the health ministry, I inquired about the status of the URS repair work, and I was told that it would begin in 2005.

Separately, on April 30, 2003, USAID awarded Abt Associates, a Boston-based health care consultancy, a contract worth between $10 million and $43.8 million to "ensure the rapid normalization of health services in Iraq while strengthening the overall health system in the country." I asked for an interview with Abt staff in Iraq in March 2004 but my request was turned down by Keith Collins, the company public relations liaison. As it turned out, the staff members weren't on the ground. Once military offensives in Fallujah, Kerbala, and Najaf got under way and the hostage takings began in April 2004, Abt's international staff fled the country.

Most curious however, was that out of thirty-five health system officials I interviewed, including the heads of four Baghdad hospitals, only three people were aware of Abt. The deputy minister thought they were a nonprofit of some kind (Abt is one of the world's largest for-profit health consultancy, according to its own Web site);[119] the head of the state pharmaceutical company said that he had attended a training seminar that they had conducted; and the director of the Basra maternity and pediatric hospital remembered having been interviewed by them about his hospital's needs, after which they failed to return.[120]

Abt Associates' Web site claims that it has seven offices in Iraq and that it works in four basic areas: strengthening the Ministry of Health, training health professionals, delivering equipment to public health clinics, and distributing small grants to Iraqi and other organizations such as the Iraqi Nurses Association (INA). Through Abt, INA was given money to hold a two-day conference and $137,000 to buy new uniforms, bed linens, and nurses' kits at the Yarmouk hospital.[121]

The company also says it is piloting a rapid-response disease surveillance system in Basra and parts of Baghdad. The system is being designed to report on selected communicable diseases with real-time data entry and information availability. Initially, telephone reporting was to be the method to immediately enter reportable diseases in parallel with a networked data entry system.

The project would have sounded hilarious to most health care workers were the situation not so tragic. There is no intercom system at any of the hospitals, let alone pagers. Few have telephones apart from the MCI phones issued to the hospital directors, which cannot call ordinary Iraqi telephones. Yet a few doctors have private Iraqna cell phones that they pay for out of their own pockets by working at private clinics in the afternoons and evenings. Dr. Awqati explained that the only way that doctors communicate under normal circumstances or even during emergencies is by physically walking (or running) from one ward to the next.

A little investigation on the Internet turned up some interesting ties. Abt Vice President for International Development Janet Ballantyne, the woman in charge of the Iraq project, joined Abt in the fall of 2002, and had previously served as counselor and acting deputy administrator at USAID—making me wonder if there wasn't a pattern here. After all, Creative Associates had similar ties to USAID. From 1996 to 1999, Ballantyne was the USAID mission director for Russia, a position she also held in Nicaragua from 1990 to 1994. She was previously professor of National Strategic Policy Studies at the National War College.[122]

On April 30, 2004, in her new post, Ballantyne was in

Zurich, Switzerland, giving a lecture to "influential" health care professionals from thirty-one countries, according to the company Web site. "No matter your politics, there were clearly healthcare needs in Iraq after the war. Abt Associates has been there from the beginning of reconstruction, and we have developed a model for dealing with post-conflict healthcare system restoration that really works." At the time of her lecture, most of Abt's international staff had spent much of the previous month outside Iraq because of the security situation.

NGOS ABANDON WORK

I don't want to suggest that no change is taking place in the health care system. Some say the situation is uniformly worse; most say it has improved somewhat. There are no longer bans on the importation of medicines, and some repair and new construction is under way. However, the reconstruction is not being done by American companies, but by bilateral donors from other countries such as Japan, Korea, and Spain.

Most disheartening is that many of the international NGOs who had been working in Iraq for over a decade have quietly curtailed their activities, some out of frustration with the new ministry, others because of security concerns. For one, the ministry is controlled by a single party, the Islamic Daawa party, an anticommunist group with close links to Iran. Party members blew up the Iraqi Ministry of Planning in 1982 in a failed effort to dislodge Saddam Hussein. Ammar al Saffar, the deputy minister of health, told me that he had returned to Iraq to take part in electoral politics only to be drafted into working at the ministry in a job that he had little experience with. "I don't know how I found myself in this ocean. I have to swim but the current is very strong," he said.[123]

I met with Yarub al-Shiraida, international projects coordinator for LIFE, an Iraqi American/Canadian foundation that has been working in Iraq for over a decade. They were promised $15,000 from Research Triangle Institute International (see chapter four) to convene doctors from every governorate in Basra to discuss the overall health sector, but the money had failed to materialize weeks after the conference had concluded its work. LIFE had slowed down its work because of the lack of funds, the security situation, and the confusion at the ministry.[124]

I also met with Hassan Rawi, architect and relief and rehabilitation manager for the International Federation of Red Cross and Red Crescent societies (IFRC). In the last few years the IFRC built forty-six primary health care centers, but it was now reduced to working on just one at the time. Trained people were scarce. Security concerns had led to the departure of their international staff, and the local staff had stopped working with the ministry because of the complete disorganization. "I went to several meetings with them in September and October but everything changed so often, we gave up. Instead we just work directly with the primary health care centers," Rawi said. When Abt took over the Iraqi health sector, the Americans had not bothered to call the IFRC. Rawi felt, given the opportunity, he could share a lot of experiences with them, largely the mistakes they had made in the past: the fact that medical kits for Basra were very different from the ones needed up north, the problems of flooding in many of the buildings that were built below the water table, etc.[125]

Further, Dr. Koresh al Qaseer, president of the Iraqi Surgeons Association suggested there were widespread problems in the health care field, saying that the situation was not looking good. "If you want to conduct an operation, you need more than just a surgeon. You need the right medicines to take care of the patient after the surgery; you need an intensive care unit on standby. The problem with George Bush is that he has neither the right medicine nor an intensive care unit for Iraq."[126]

BANKING ON EMPIRE

As Iraq slid into chaos by the spring of 2004, the only major foreign contractors to remain in the country were those financed by the U.S. military (such as Halliburton) or by USAID (such as Bechtel). In their eagerness to help out local and foreign contractors whose revenues were not directly guaranteed by the American taxpayer, the U.S. government arranged for Iraqi ministries to borrow billions of dollars to buy much-needed equipment from overseas suppliers, but only by mortgaging the national oil revenues through the Trade Bank of Iraq (TBI).

Hussein al-Uzri, president of the TBI, announced in Kuwait City in January 2004 that the bank had raised $2.4 billion in export guarantees for trade between Iraq and foreign companies and governments, and it had issued $300 million worth of letters of credit.[127]

The TBI was formed partially to replace the trade guarantees established by the United Nations oil-for-food program, imposed on Iraq in 1995 during the sanctions regime against Saddam Hussein. The program provided a means of controlling Iraq's purchase of humanitarian goods from other countries in exchange for Iraqi petroleum, while prohibiting the purchase of goods that could theoretically be used for military purposes. The oil-for-food program, which in total used $46 billion in Iraqi export earnings, was brought to an end in November 2003.

Unlike the oil-for-food program, the guarantees of the TBI are administered not by an UN agency, but by the private sector and its allies in various national governments. The export credits were to provide backing for purchases of raw materials, medical supplies, bulk food imports, fertilizer, and capital equipment. Like the Iraq reconstruction contracts that have favored U.S. companies with political connections, the export credits of the TBI favor companies from contributing nations, whether or not their products are cheap or well made.

Take the case of the U.S. export credit agency that initially underwrote the TBI. "Those oil revenues will be used to support the Iraq Trade Bank letters of credit," said David Chavern, a senior official with ExIm addressing attendees at a recent briefing in Washington, D.C. organized by Equity International for potential investors in Iraq. "And we will ensure those letters of credit for the US exporter."[128]

Of the $2.4 billion that the TBI secured in export guarantees, ExIm approved $500 million in letters of credit. The money from ExIm ensured that the investments of U.S. corporations in Iraq were risk free. If Iraqi ministries defaulted on any of their payments to U.S. companies, ExIm would be required to pay in their place. Then ExIm would take its money back from Iraq's Development Fund, the acting budget for Iraq that is 95 percent made up of oil revenues, which in turn was under occupation control.

Other members of the occupation coalition contributed

too. Japan's export credit agency, NEXI, provided $500 million, the Italian SACE contributed $300 million, while export credit agencies from thirteen other European countries were also contributors.

"Without the agreement with these export credit agencies, the Trade Bank of Iraq would have had to concentrate exclusively on state purchases," said Marek Belka, the head of economic policy in Iraq's temporary administration. "Iraqis at the moment have to pay cash for pretty much everything, which is hugely cumbersome and risky. The fact that the Trade Bank of Iraq can now issue letters of credit will make it easy for Iraqis to buy goods in a more civilized and safer fashion. It will also reduce their costs."[129]

But critics say that the occupation authorities and multinational banks may be shackling a future Iraqi government with an unknown quantity of debt to these occupation-favored suppliers. Open government advocates have also complained that the Iraqi Development Fund lacks transparency and decisions concerning the fund are not subject to scrutiny or public comment. Thus the U.S. could choose to set the rules to pay itself back, using money from Iraqi oil to do it. "The oil figures are very murky and secretive," Nomi Prins former investment banker and author of *Other People's Money: The Corporate Mugging of America* told Mitch Jeserich of Free Speech Radio News. "That same oil for which no one has the appropriate...information is being used to collateralize multiple things. You're effectively leveraging oil for which the revenues are non-transparent."

The management contract for the TBI, worth $2 million over 2.5 years, was awarded to a consortium of thirteen banks representing fourteen countries, led by JP Morgan Chase, in July 2003, after a competitive bidding process against four other international consortia. (New York-based JP Morgan Chase was formed from the merger in December 2000 of one of the world's largest commercial banks, Chase Manhattan Corporation, and the investment bank JP Morgan & Company.) Here critics noted that the arrival of JP Morgan Chase marked the possible takeover of Iraq's banking system by foreign banks. Two months after the establishment of the Trade Bank of Iraq, the occupation authorities enacted Order 39: the opening up of all of Iraq's resources to foreign ownership except for oil. Shortly afterwards, the appointed Iraqi finance minister, Kamel al-Gailani, began major reforms to Iraq's banking system, such as allowing foreign financial corporations to own 100 percent of the banks in Iraq. The move marked the first time since the 1950s that foreign banks will have access to Iraq's financial system, whose main asset is the second largest oil reserves in the world.

According to Prins, the foreign ownership of Iraqi banks makes it practically impossible for locally owned banks to participate in the forging of a new economy. The Iraqi banks that are able to avoid a foreign takeover now have to compete with foreign banks and their many subsidiaries that have an unlimited source of capital and lending abilities.

"Are these the kind of laws that help Iraq rebuild for Iraqis or are these the kind of laws that open Iraq up for corporations to come in and profit off of Iraq's resources?" asked Rania Masri, program director with the Institute on Southern Studies and codirector of the Campaign to Stop the War Profiteers. "It reeks of colonialism. It does not represent a rebuilding."

SERVICING DESPOTISM

Indeed, JP Morgan Chase was no stranger to the architects of the occupation, being the seventh-largest career patron of Dick Cheney over the last twenty years.[130] The bank fitted right into occupied Iraq, given that it already had close relationships with companies that have received billions of dollars' worth of contracts there. On JP Morgan Chase's board of directors sits Riley Bechtel, CEO of Bechtel. Another notable on JP Morgan Chase's board is Lee Raymond, the chairman of the board of Exxon Mobil Corporation.[131]

Lest critics suggest that JP Morgan Chase is unqualified to run Iraq's banking system, it must be said that the company does have experience working in the Middle East. Chase has been assisting Qatar's national bank for the past thirty years by managing the country's export of oil and natural gas, thus making Qatar one of the wealthiest countries in the region and helping to solidify Qatar's monarchy.[132]

Qatar is just one of several nondemocratic regimes that JP Morgan Chase has given financial assistance to. In fact, the company has a long history of working with unethical regimes, spanning U.S. slavery to the Enron scandal. A study by California's insurance commissioner showed the former company Chase, which is now a part of JP Morgan Chase, as one of several insurance companies that provided life insurance to slave owners for their slaves. When a slave died, according to the study, Chase paid the slave owner for the loss. The bank has never paid reparations and JP Morgan Chase's spokesperson Charlotte Gilbert-Biro said, "We don't believe there's any basis for liability on the part of the bank."[133] And luckily for the Nazis in World War II, Chase National Bank and JP Morgan both assisted the Third Reich by seizing the bank accounts of Jewish customers, whose assets they did not return after the war. A 1945 U.S. Treasury Department report on U.S. banking activities during the war stated that the "record of the [Chase] Paris branch is one of uncalled-for responsiveness to the desires of the Germans and an apparent desire to enhance its influence with them."[134]

JP Morgan and Chase's history of unsavory assistance of racist governments is not limited to the U.S. and Europe. The company has been the subject of a lawsuit for providing financial assistance to South Africa's apartheid government to expand its police and security apparatus, even after the United Nations urged a boycott of the racist government in 1964, declaring apartheid a crime against humanity. JP Morgan refused to comment on the case, as it was still under litigation at the time of writing.[135]

More recently, in 2002, the U.S. Securities and Exchange Commission indicted JP Morgan Chase for assisting Enron to manipulate its financial records. And a Senate committee found that JP Morgan Chase, along with Citigroup, knew the money they were giving to Enron was used to manipulate its financial statements rather than meet its legal business goals. This manipulation left Californians with skyrocketing power bills while at the same time causing rolling power outages throughout the state.[136]

INTERNATIONAL FINANCE CORPORATION

Besides export credits, other new sources of capital for Iraq have been proposed. Although, given the security situation in Iraq, it remains to be seen if these promises will be fulfilled. In mid-March 2004, the International Finance Corporation (IFC), a division of the World Bank, was planning to venture into Iraq by June 2004, according to Assaad

Jabre, vice-president of operations. Of the $200 million that the IFC offered, a technical assistance component of up to $30 million was earmarked for capacity building of other sectors while the $170 million was scheduled for small and medium enterprise. Jabre told reporters, "We are open to investing in any sectors of the economy in Iraq, provided they are viable projects. At this point of time Iraq has huge investment potential however good governance is equally important factor in development of Iraq."[137]

BARONS OF BAGHDAD

Investment in Iraq, however, is not entirely limited to foreign companies. According to a report by the Center for International Private Enterprise, a nonprofit affiliate of the U.S. Chamber of Commerce, Iraq has twelve powerful family groups that have capitalized a variety of sectors in Iraq over several decades. Some of their histories can be found in a book titled *The Old Social Classes and the Revolutionary Movement of Iraq* by Hanna Batatu that was published in the United States in 1978. Yet, the book does not include those Iraqis who emerged as the new merchant class under Saddam Hussein's patronage. Presumably the dynasties described by Batatu will enjoy greater favor with the administration than those Saddam-era companies.

"With business contacts throughout the Gulf and the Middle East and extending into Europe, Iraq has developed its own powerful set of oligarchs. The al-Bunnias, al-Khudairys, and Kubbas have become the region's own Rockefellers, Gettys, and Fords. Like their American counterparts, these Iraqi dynasties are built on property, construction, technology, and manufacturing and are over a cen-

tury old," wrote Adrian Gatton and Clayton Hirst in the
Independent of London, in February 2004.[138]

Gatton and Hirst say that the al-Bunnia family is one of
the oldest and arguably one of the most powerful in Iraq.
The Bunnia industrial group is headed by Abdul Wahab
Mahmoud al Bunnia, who is grooming his son, Khalil, to
take over. Founded in 1910, the business now has four thousand staff members and over forty subsidiaries involved in
construction, food, banking, insurance, textiles, and hotels.
Like most successful Iraqi families, it is developing links
with Western companies. It owns a Pepsi bottling factory, a
BMW dealership, and also claims to have agreements with
IBM, Hyundai, and Epson. Some members of the al-Bunnia
family are known to lavish their riches on luxury goods.
Khalil recently boasted he possessed a collection of "the
most expensive cars in the world." Incidentally, Sadoon al-
Bunnia, one of three principals of the company, is also a
founding partner of a Swiss-registered firm called the
Malaysian Swiss Gulf and African Chamber (MIGA), which
the U.S. government and the United Nations Security
Council have designated as funders of al Qaeda.[139]

The al-Bunnias helped Bechtel complete the building of
the Al Mat bypass, about 110 miles from the Jordanian border, near the town of Ar Rutbah, that was destroyed by
bombing during the invasion. A fifty-man team from the
Iraqi company worked seven days a week in 110-degree heat
to complete it in less than a month.[140]

(When I learned that the al-Bunnias were one of Bechtel's
first subcontractors, I requested an interview with the company. I spent three fruitless occasions waiting in the lobby of
the company's office, plus several rather expensive satellite
phone calls, but the closest I got to seeing the inside of the

company was an escorted trip to the second floor restroom. However, the company did send me an unexpected and very nice email greeting for the New Year, after I left the country in December 2003.)

Rivaling al-Bunnia is the al-Khudairy dynasty, which is run by Adnan al-Khudairy, who is also chairman of the Iraqi Contractors Federation. According to Gatton and Hirst, the family controls one of the largest construction companies in the region and owns the country's largest drug firm, Dhofar. Employing five thousand, its tentacles extend to the West, notably as party to a joint venture with U.K. oil company Wood Group and U.S. construction firm Shaw Group. The family has been critical of the occupation authorities. At last year's World Economic Forum, Faisal al-Khudairy, Dhofar's chairman, accused it of "rehiring tainted government officials."

The Khawwam al Abdul Abbas family is another powerful bunch. On December 2, 2003, a contract to run a new Iraqi airline named al Iraqiyya Air was signed by Fakher Fareg Mohammed, the general director of the civil aviation authority in the Ministry of Transport, with three members of the Khawwam family. The ministry's share in the company's capital was to be $25 million (under 25 percent), which would be paid from the assets of the old Iraqi Airways.

An exposè in *Al Mu'tamar*, the Iraqi National Congress (INC) daily newspaper, reprinted documents from Saddam Hussein's presidential office outlining the Khawwam al Abdul Abbas family's dealings with the former dictator. The family was said to run two front companies, Al Huda and Alia, for Saddam's regime. Al Huda was a partner of the Iraqi State Oil Marketing Organization that has been implicated in the smuggling of oil under the sanctions. The newspaper printed photocopies of documents disclosing how the family was involved in oil smuggling, bribing of Iraqi and non-Iraqi officials, and importing expired food items to Iraq under the oil-for-food program.[141]

Then there is the Kubba group. Founded in 1953 and run by Hikmet Hadi Kubba, the family run company has gained respectability though charity. Its Kubba Foundation aims to "promote the education, health, and general welfare of Iraqis." The family has ventures in information technology, marketing, telecoms, engineering, and construction. It owns Kufa Cola as well as Babil soft drinks, which is involved in a joint venture with Pepsi, and the Basra and Tikrit dairies. The Kubba Web site makes no secret of the company's desire to cash in on the confusion that ensued after the fall of Saddam, boasting that it is "well-positioned to help international businesses navigate through the myriad of commercial and political complexities facing the Iraqi market today."[142]

Also in the big league is the Munir Sukhtian family, which began its enterprise in 1933 when it set up as a pharmacy in Tulkarem, Palestine. Today, the company is run by the founder's three sons, and much of its business is in Jordan, spanning telecoms, chemicals, pharmaceuticals, and manufacturing. The other Iraqi families, such as Shanshal, al-Dulaimi, and al-Kharbeet, avoid publicity and less is known about their dealings.[143]

CONCLUSION

It is very difficult to draw immediate conclusions about the success or failure of the reconstruction. Both critics and supporters abound. The military, USAID, and the occupation authorities have often listed their achievements, and while some of them are questionable, many are honest efforts to provide important services to ordinary Iraqis. (One such questionable achievement is girls attending school. Girls attended school under Saddam Hussein. His regime was one of the most permissive on women's rights in the region. If anything the number of girls in schools has probably dropped because of the current security threats.) The American taxpayer who is currently footing the bill, may quibble about the price tag, but the real question is what ordinary Iraqis think about the results.

A poll conducted by the one-year-old Iraq Centre for Research and Strategic Studies, released in late May 2004, showed that 90 percent of the Iraqi population viewed U.S. forces as occupiers, not liberators, and nearly 70 percent backed Moqtada al Sadr to some degree. More than half of a representative sample—comprising sixteen hundred Shiite and Sunni Arabs and Kurds polled in all of Iraq's main regions—wanted occupation troops to leave Iraq, compared to about 20 percent polled in an October survey.[144]

Most Iraqis, even those who strongly supported American intervention, are not satisfied. Indeed many are downright angry at the lack of basic services such as electricity and telephones. They fear the uncertain future held out in the privitization of Iraqi industries and hope for an end to the chaos in the hospitals, and most importantly, the growing danger in the streets.

CHAPTER THREE

Soldiers of Fortune

Man Bahadur Gurung fingered his machine gun a little nervously. The view from the eighteenth floor of the Sheraton, one of the tallest buildings in Baghdad, was spectacular, despite the fact that most of the city had no electricity and that only wealthy homes and businesses equipped with generators lit up the night. Behind him, Halliburton employees chatted over dinner. Stepping out of the elevator, I noticed he eyed me with apprehension. I wore no badge and looked generally out of place.

Gurung, I learned, was formerly a Gurkha soldier—one of a long line of soldiers for hire. In 1817, the British army first employed Gurkhas, hardy Nepalis from the Himalayas, as a local supply of hired guns. Gurung works for the Armor Group, one of dozens of security companies in the country. His firm was hired by Halliburton to guard the employees who live in the Sheraton tower. Gurung was far from home, but this wasn't his first time away. He had worked previously in war-torn Sierra Leone and in Angola, guarding Ranger oil facilities.[145] I asked if I could get a drink at the café and he reluctantly agreed to call over a Halliburton employee.

The answer was an emphatic no, and so he asked me to leave, gesturing with his gun towards the elevator. I turned to leave, stepping back into the elevator. On my descent I noticed Gurung's colleagues stationed on every floor from the penthouse through the eighth. Sporting the blue uniform of the Armor Group, a flak jacket, and a machine gun, the Gurkhas stood watch.

The next day, across town in the basement of the convention center where Bechtel has its offices, we met Maniram Gurung, another Gurkha, outside the United States Consul's Office. Standing in front of photographs of Bush, Cheney, and Powell, Gurung watched American soldiers, Iraqi government officials, and contractors hurry by, conversing on the business of nation building. But he was not a member of the occupation forces—his red badge identified him as an employee of another private security company called Global Risk.[146]

For both these Gurkha riflemen, Iraq guard duty was yet another boring but well-paying job, allowing them to send thirteen hundred dollars home to their families every month. It wasn't as much as they used to earn in the British army (twenty-five hundred dollars a month in 1990), but it helped pay the bills, and there were some advantages—these jobs last only six months; whereas the British army postings in exotic locales like Brunei and Hong Kong allowed for visits home only once every three years. Maniram Gurung told me that his group is confined to their barracks at night, eight men to a trailer home, and food is strictly "English" (a euphemism to mean Western), provided by Halliburton sweatshop cooks from India whose base pay was just three dollars a day.

While guards like Gurung make a princely salary by

Middle Eastern standards, their Iraqi counterparts make far less. Mohammed al-Husany, the ever cheerful head of security at the barricades outside the Palestine and Sheraton hotels, told me that he made just one hundred dollars a month, not enough to support his wife and two kids, but better than nothing in a country with an estimated 70 percent rate of unemployment. "I want a job with the American companies. I have a second degree black belt in karate, and I know how to fire every kind of weapon. AK-47s, M-16s, all of them. But my friends who work for Halliburton's security make four hundred dollars a month and the American and European security guards even more," he confided in me.[147]

Later I ran into two burly men with large two-way radios and guns waiting calmly outside an Internet cafe. As I left the room, I noticed that they looked European and wore matching casual light green clothing. Stopping to chat I asked them where they were from. "Trade delegation, sir," said one with an English accent. The other had a strong Scottish accent and his open flak jacket revealed a logo on his shirt that read "Olive Security."[148]

MEN WITH GUNS

Indeed it is hard not to notice the poker-faced men with guns patrolling every sensitive location in Iraq. Unofficial estimates of the number of these ex-soldiers for hire suggest that there are twenty thousand armed men (and a few women too) in Iraq providing security services to private companies, government facilities, and the occupation forces. The vast majority of this guard is made up of Iraqis who earn between sixty and two hundred dollars a month performing a function not that different from bank guards in any other country in the world. A contract that I was shown from Group 4 Falck, a British security company, offered two armed guards twenty-four hours a day for any building for $6106 a month, of which the Iraqi guards' salaries amounted to just 10 percent.[149]

Above Iraqis on the pay scale are ex-soldiers from Nepal, India, and Fiji. Next on the pay scale are Chilean, South African, and ex–Soviet bloc personnel. Finally there are the highly trained ex-Special Forces people from Britain and the United States who are paid much, much more—in some cases over one thousand dollars a day. These men guard high-profile targets and train American and Iraqi military and police in defensive and offensive tactics. While most of these men and women try to stay out of combat, they have been known to engage in military action.

Olive Security from Mayfair, London, was one of the first security companies on the ground in Iraq, arriving immediately after the troops. The company, created by Harry Legge-Bourke, the brother of the former nanny to Princes William and Harry, draws off a pool of more than one hundred former Special Air Services (SAS) soldiers (the elite British regiment, similar to the Special Forces) for use as bodyguards and to prepare logistical reports on the security situation. Two days after the invasion was complete, the firm deployed thirty-eight former SAS officers to set up operational centers for Bechtel. At the time, Legge-Bourke said: "This is crisis management in a hostile environment. You need people who know what they are doing."[150]

Soon hundreds of out-of-work ex-soldiers from India to Chile and South Africa to Fiji were flooding into the country. As K. P. Saidalavi, general secretary of the National Ex-servicemen Coordination Committee in Kerala, India, told the *Hindu* newspaper about the Indian recruits, "Many of these ex-soldiers are well aware of the risks involved in such jobs, but they are forced to take . . . them [up] because they don't get a job that pays at least Rs. 2,000 [forty dollars] a month."

The security recruitment was done through a company at Karikkamuri in Kochi, Kerala (where English is widely spoken) under the guise of selecting security guards for a Kuwaiti firm that supplies workers to U.S. forces in the Gulf for salaries ranging from one thousand to twenty-five hundred dollars together with all transportation, meals, and accommodation.[151]

Hundreds of recruits came from Fiji, under the leadership of Major Kelevi Vakasavuwaqa, to work for Global Risk. Recruiting agent, Lieutenant Colonel Sakiusa Raivoce, told the local paper that this job was much better than the peacekeeping services. "In Lebanon and Sinai, our soldiers stand in the hot sun and out in the open. They are always exposed to risk, but in Iraq, it will be different. Working conditions will be so good.... The response has been overwhelming and I think [soldiers] really want to go so that they can help their families," he said. One of the soldiers who took up the job offer was Ratendra Nath Sharma, a taxi driver in Nadi. "I understand the risk involved but it will be, if not better, similar to the conditions in the Middle East. I believe this is also an opportunity of a lifetime for me."[152]

TOP OF THE LINE SERVICE FROM THE BRITISH

Perhaps the most expensive of these security contractors are the British companies. David Claridge, managing director of the London-based Janusian Security Risk Management, told the *Chicago Tribune* that clients can expect to pay up to ten thousand dollars a day for top-of-the-line service that would include four armed guards and two armored vehicles. Some employees can make as much as five hundred to two thousand dollars a day, depending on training and job.

He explained that these companies structure their organization very much like the military—giving employees "ranks" based on experience and training. They own military equipment such as Kiowa Warrior helicopters and they train their pilots to fly them in Iraqi skies, deploying for months on end, training at military installations, and working daily with U.S. commanders in any given war zone.

John Davidson, who runs Rubicon International, a British security company whose interests in Iraq include contracts with BP and Motorola, told the *Scotsman* newspaper that they prefer to hire former members of Britain's special forces, the SAS. "The SAS are extremely well-trained, low-profile, not waving flags. They go about things in a quiet manner, they are the crème de la crème," he said.

These men can earn as much as a $250,000 a year—about three times as much as than they can earn in Britain—guarding terrified American businessmen working in Iraq. The boom in Iraq has even caused a small crisis for the British security forces. The *Scotsman* estimates that one in six SAS and SBS (Special Boat Service) men have asked for permission to quit their jobs to go to Iraq. The British government is alarmed by the trend because it costs them as much as $3 million to train each of these men.[153]

Protected by these gun-toting private security guards, U.S. and European businessmen were soon crisscrossing the country in what has become the unofficial transportation of the war profiteers: shiny, new white GMC Suburban Blazers.

CLEAN, CORPORATE AND EFFICIENT

But private security in Iraq goes far beyond mere security guards in SUVs. Within days of the occupation, an unnamed Pentagon official told *The New York Times* that they were seeking something more than the United Nations peace-keeping troops to secure post-Saddam Iraq. "We know we want something a little more corporate and more efficient with cleaner lines of authority and responsibility, " said the official.[154]

On April 7, 2003, two days before Iraq was officially "liberated," I received an anonymous tip-off that a company called Dyncorp was looking for police trainers. When I called the number given me by the informant, I was connected to an office just outside Forth Worth, Texas, where recruiters were answering the phones. "When the area is safe, we will go in. Watch CNN. In the meantime, fax us a resume if you want a job," Homer Newman, a Dyncorp recruiter told me.[155]

Newman directed me to a Web site (http://www.police-mission.com/iraq.asp) that informed me that Dyncorp was looking for "individuals with appropriate experience and expertise to participate in an international effort to re-establish police, justice and prison functions in post-conflict Iraq." The company is looking for active duty or recently retired cops and prison guards and "experienced judicial experts." Applicants, the site stated, must be U.S. citizens with ten years of sworn civilian domestic law enforcement.

Surprised, I called Chuck Wilkins, a company spokesman in Virginia, to ask him if the company had won a contract. His response was terse. "The contract hasn't yet been awarded," he said.[156] Ten days after my phone call, Dyncorp was awarded the police-training contract.[157] Obviously the company was well positioned to know about and win the contract all along—they had been providing security guards under contract to the U.S. military in Kuwait for several years.[158]

ALLEGED HUMAN RIGHTS VIOLATIONS AND FRAUD

Dyncorp has plenty of experience in the rent-a-cop field in other hot spots: armed Dyncorp employees make up the core of the police force in Bosnia; Dyncorp troops protect Afghan president Hamid Karzai and Dyncorp planes and pilots fly defoliation missions over coca crops in Colombia, spraying peasants with toxins in the process. Back home in the United States, Dyncorp is in charge of the border posts between the United States and Mexico. The company oversees many of the Pentagon's weapons-testing ranges, staffs the entire Air Force One fleet of presidential planes and helicopters, and reviews security clearance applications of military and civilian personnel for the navy.[159]

Dyncorp was founded in 1946 as a project of a small group of returning World War II pilots seeking to use their military contacts to make a living in the air cargo business. Named California Eastern Airways, the original company was soon airlifting supplies to Asia for use in the Korean War. By 2002, Dyncorp, headquartered in Reston, Virginia, was the nation's thirteenth largest military contractor with $2.3 billion in revenue. The week that the Iraq jobs were posted, the company merged with Computer Sciences Corporation, an El Segundo, California-based technology services company, in an acquisition worth nearly $1 billion.[160]

As I stated earlier, the company is never far from controversy. Under the Plan Colombia contract, the company had
88 aircraft and 307 employees—139 of them American—flying missions to eradicate coca fields in Colombia. *Soldier of
Fortune* magazine once ran a cover story on Dyncorp, pro-
claiming it "Colombia's Coke-Dustin' Broncos."[161] But U.S.
Representative Janice Schakowsky, an Illinois Democrat,
told *Wired* magazine that hiring a private company to fly
what amounts to combat missions is asking for trouble.
"Dyncorp's employees have a history of behaving like cow-
boys," Schakowsky noted. "Is the U.S. military privatizing
its missions to avoid public controversy or to avoid embar-
rassment—to hide body bags from the media and shield the
military from public opinion?" she asked.[162]

Indeed a group of Ecuadorian peasants filed a class action
against the company in September 2001. The suit alleges that
herbicides spread by Dyncorp in Colombia were drifting
across the border, withering legitimate crops, causing human
and livestock illness, and, in several cases, killing children.
Assistant Secretary of State Rand Beers intervened in the
case right away telling the judge the lawsuit posed "a grave
risk to U.S. national security and foreign policy objectives."

What's more, Kathryn Bolkovac, a UN International
Police Force monitor, filed a lawsuit in Britain, in 2001,
against Dyncorp for unfair dismissal after she reported that
Dyncorp police trainers in Bosnia were paying for prostitutes
and participating in sex trafficking. Many of the Dyncorp
employees were forced to resign under suspicion of illegal
activity. But none was prosecuted, as they all enjoyed immunity in Bosnia.

Earlier that year Ben Johnston, a Dyncorp aircraft
mechanic for Apache and Blackhawk helicopters in Kosovo,

filed a lawsuit against his employer. The suit alleged that in the latter part of 1999 Johnson "learned that employees and supervisors from Dyncorp were engaging in perverse, illegal and inhumane behavior [and] were purchasing illegal weapons, women, forged passports and [participating in] other immoral acts." The suit charges that "Johnston witnessed coworkers and supervisors literally buying and selling women for their own personal enjoyment, and employees would brag about the various ages and talents of the individual slaves they had purchased." "Dyncorp is just as immoral and elite as possible, and any rule they can break they do," Johnston told *Insight* magazine.

He also charged that the company billed the army for unnecessary repairs and padded the payroll. "What they say in Bosnia is that Dyncorp just needs a warm body—that's the Dyncorp slogan. Even if you don't do an eight-hour day, they'll sign you in for it because that's how they bill the government. It's a total fraud."[163]

WE RULE! YOU FOLLOW ORDERS

Dyncorp attracted a mixture of ordinary policemen from the United States who jumped at the opportunity to double their salaries, as well as quite a few *Soldier of Fortune* magazine readers—macho, swaggering types who walked around Iraq wearing Oakley sunglasses, Kevlar helmets, and flak jackets, thinking that they owned the place.

The most detailed independent description of Dyncorp employees comes from Tucker Carlson, a journalist from *Esquire* magazine who traveled with a Dyncorp contingent for a couple of weeks in December, witnessing some pretty disturbing incidents along the way.

Just south of Nasiriyah, we stopped for gas. Thanks
to sabotaged oil pipelines and a huge glut of new
vehicles (more than three hundred thousand since
the war), every station has a gas line. Some are more
than a mile long. People can wait for days, camped
out in their cars, for a full tank. We had no intention of doing that. Waiting in line, stationary and
exposed, was simply too dangerous. Instead, we
commandeered the gas station.

All four vehicles roared in at high speed. Two
went directly to the pumps. Two formed mobile
roadblocks near the entrance. Contractors with
guns jumped out and stopped traffic from coming
in. Others took positions around the perimeter of
the station. Kelly motioned for me to stand guard
with my rifle by the back wall. There was a large
and growing crowd around us. It looked hostile.

And no wonder. We'd swooped in and stolen
their places in line, reminding them, as if they
needed it, of the oldest rule there is: Armed people
get to do exactly what they want; everyone else has
to shut up and take it.[164]

Carlson thus described some of the more obnoxious contractors that he met:

There are civilians toting guns in Iraq who should-
n't be. Some of them are easy to spot. I ran into one
late one night outside the Gardenia Hotel, a dumpy
former office building.

Kelly and I were staying in a house across the
street, and I'd walked over to see if I could find

someone to do my laundry. Standing on the front
steps was a middle-aged Englishman. He introduced
himself as Richard, a former member of the 22nd
SAS. He had a rifle slung over his shoulder, and he
was slobbering drunk. Hearing my accent, he
immediately lit into Americans as fearful and
weak. "Come with me, my Yankee Doodle Dandy
wanker," he said. "I'll take you places you've never
been."

Like where? I said. He looked as if he were about
to tell me. Then he stopped and lurched forward,
almost on top of me. "You're not Irish, are you?" he
demanded, breathing in my face. Nope. "Good
man!" He all but embraced me. He'd killed enough
of the Irish in Ulster, he said. He'd hate to have to
do it again.

About ten days after I left Iraq, Richard put three
bullets into a man he was supposed to be protecting. Apparently, it was an accident. He'd forgotten
to take his rifle off automatic and . . . well, you
know. The man survived. Richard was fired. It
turned out he had never served in the SAS.[165]

(The security contractors are equal opportunity employ-
ers, though. Derek William Adgey, a Royal Marine from
Belfast, jailed for four years for helping the Ulster Freedom
Fighters, was hired by Armor Group to guard Bechtel
employees. He was subsequently suspended when the
Belfast Telegraph published details of his past.)[166]

According to Carlson, sometimes the Dyncorp contractors simply took the law into their own hands.

One night in December, two Dyncorp contractors caught a man they'd been looking for outside the Baghdad Hotel. According to local witnesses, the man had kidnapped several children and attempted to sell them. The contractors reduced him to a bloody mound before turning "what was left of him" over to the Iraqi police. They told me about it at breakfast the next morning. They looked pleased... Of course, contractors aren't always high minded. With no one watching, it's tempting to settle scores. The week before I arrived, Sean Penn came to Iraq on some sort of special assignment for the *San Francisco Chronicle*. The actor was getting out of a cab in downtown Baghdad when a group of contractors spotted him. The contractors didn't share Penn's politics. Plus, they found the idea of him annoying. So they took his camera and made him stand in the rain for forty-five minutes while they ran an imaginary security check on his equipment. There was nothing Penn could do about it. They had guns. He didn't. Tough luck.[167]

SCARED OUT OF THEIR MINDS

This situation changed rapidly. I made a trip to Baghdad in April 2004, two weeks after the Blackwater employees were strung up in Fallujah, and the contrast with my December 2003 trip was startling. The daily parade of men with guns, flak jackets, and Kevlar helmets that I had witnessed every morning around the Sheraton was no longer in evidence. Once Iraqis started fighting back, targeting the contractors, the macho men went into shock and disappeared. All of a sudden the swagger was gone.

Roger Carpenter, a Kansas recruit for Dyncorp, had come to Iraq on March 17, 2004 to help teach self-defense and police techniques to Iraqi police and bodyguard recruits. Interviewed in the *Wichita Eagle*, his hometown newspaper, almost a month later, he said he hadn't made it out of the Al Sadeer hotel in Baghdad, which was surrounded by wire, barricades, and machine gun emplacements. "Hotel doesn't quite describe it. It's now more like a fortress," he said.[168]

Another description came from an engineer working in a northern city, who had this to say about the Dyncorp contractors they hired: "They are a bunch of unsure to outright shit scared [people] and [they] drive like maniacs. Have secured the [company name deleted] crew in camp with no move until we can resolve how the [security] convoys are run because they are and will continue to piss the locals off more each day until they try killing everyone. Dyncorp would take the cake for being the most unprofessional crews I have had the displeasure to meet out here. They have a few good lads but they last a few days."[169]

KURDS VERSUS ARABS

By April 2004, the anniversary of liberation, Dyncorp wasn't the only contractor to come under fire. A South African security company called Erinys runs the second largest training scheme in the country to create a private security force guarding the oil pipelines and refineries.

I took a trip to the main oil refinery in Baghdad, a landmark, recognizable from most parts of the city by the huge orange flare that hangs over its smokestacks all day and all night. Outside the facility, armed Iraqi guards in shiny new blue uniforms, manufactured by Cartier, warded off curious passersby. "Sorry, you have to get permission from the oil ministry," said Amir Jajw, one of the guards, waving me away. His shoulder sported two yellow stripes, the insignia of Erinys.

But I had clearance, so I got past the gates and headed inside where I was greeted by the refinery manager Dathar al-Kashab. When the Americans took over the city in April 2003, he told me, he armed his employees to defend the refinery from the looters. He continued,

> When the U.S. Army came in, I went out and talked to the commander and said, "Now [the oil refinery] is your baby. You have to protect it." The commander said, "It's not my duty. I [have] got some other thing to do. I'm just checking, inspecting, and searching." So I said, "This is a very dangerous area. If you don't protect it, be sure that the looters will burn the refinery. My god, you have millions of liters of hydrocarbon products and hundreds of thousands of toxic chemicals. If they catch fire, you have a problem of evacuating half of Baghdad."[170]

Other oil facilities were not as well protected initially—pipelines and offices in both the north and the south of Iraq have been frequent targets of looters and saboteurs but the number of attacks has diminished as Erinys hired and trained over fourteen thousand guards around the country.

On a trip to the northern oil fields in Kirkuk, I spent time with one of the Erinys guards, Mamand Kesnazani, a Kurdish Sufi. He was a *peshmerga* (which means "ready to die" in Kurdish—the accepted name for the Kurdish fighters in northern Iraq who battled Saddam Hussein's army for decades) for Jalal Talabani's Patriotic Union of Kurdistan (PUK). Kesnazani eschewed the blue uniform, choosing instead to wear the *khaffiya* (checkered black and white headscarf) and *sharwal* (baggy pants) typical of *peshmerga* fighters.

"I've had a lot of bosses this year. First it was the PUK; then the U.S. Army came with Kellogg Brown & Root. Now the company has changed again to a British company called Erinys—it doesn't matter who it is, we are willing to defend the oil. If they pay us, that's even better," he said.[171]

Security jobs like those at Northern Oil are technically open to all Iraqis, but those staffing the checkpoint estimated 95 percent were *peshmerga*, because the occupation authorities don't trust Arabs, causing at least some bitterness among non-Kurds. A Free Speech Radio News reporter talked to a group of unemployed ex-soldiers in a primarily Shiite slum in Kirkuk, as they whiled away the afternoon drinking tea. "I went to the Coalition (the occupation authorities) to apply for a job in security," says forty-three-year-old Ibrahim al-Jaboori. "I've been a soldier my whole life and I'm 100 percent against these terrorists. But they said there are no jobs. Then I see everyone providing security is Kurdish."[172]

The top wage for rank-and-file Kurdish guards prtecting the oil fields is $120 a month, hardly a living wage. By comparison their supervisors, many of whom are South African, are estimated to earn an average salary of $5,000 a month.

THE SOUTH AFRICANS

Like Dyncorp, Erinys too has an unsavory past. Its Web site touts "management experience" in providing security services for dozens of transnational corporations, such as Ashanti Gold and BP-Amoco.

Yet in August 2003, the Wassa Association of Communities Affected by Mining (WACAM), a Ghanaian nonprofit, released a report detailing alleged human rights abuses perpetrated by Erinys workers at an Ashanti gold mine. It relays eyewitness accounts of Ashanti Gold security personnel torturing, beating, and killing local small-scale miners between 1994 and 2002. WACAM further alleges that corporate security used guard dogs to feed on trespassers.[173]

On January 28, 2004, Erinys's South African trainers came under public scrutiny when trainer Francois Strydom was killed and his colleague Deon Gouws seriously injured as a bomb exploded outside the Shaheen hotel in Baghdad. It turned out the two men had been members of South Africa's secret police in the 1980s under the apartheid regime.

Strydom was a member of Koevoet, a notoriously brutal counterinsurgency arm of the South African military that operated in Namibia during the neighboring state's fight for independence in the 1980s.[174]

Gouws was a former officer of the Vlakplaas, a secret police unit in South Africa. According to South Africa's *Sunday Times*, Gouws received an amnesty from the Truth And Reconciliation Commission after admitting to between forty and sixty petrol bombings of political activists' houses in Mamelodi, Atteridgeville, Soshanguve, Oukasie, Pietersburg, Tembisa, and Ekangala in 1986; a car bombing in 1986 that claimed the life of KwaNdebele homeland cab-

inet minister and ANC activist Piet Ntuli; and an arson
attack on the home of Mamelodi doctor Fabian Ribiero in
March 1986.[175]

Gray Branfield, another South African working for a security contractor called the Hart group, was killed in Iraq in
the town of Kut in mid-April. A couple of days later news
surfaced that he was one of South Africa's secret agents. He
had admitted to being part of a death squad that ambushed
and shot Joe Gqabi, the African National Congress's chief
representative, nineteen times as he reversed down the
driveway of his Harare home on July 31, 1981. He was a
member of the South African Defence Force's secret Project
Barnacle, a precursor to the notorious Civil Co-operation
Bureau (CCB) death squad. In 1985 he was involved in planning a raid on Gaborone in which fourteen people, including
a five-year-old child, were killed.[176]

It's not just apartheid-era killers that are heading to Iraq.
Members of the South African Police Services' elite task
force, a division of one hundred men who accompany senior
politicians like President Thabo Mbeki, are facing a severe
crisis with as many as half of their employees asking for
early retirement in order to go to Iraq. The five thousand dollars monthly salary for these men is equivalent to about six
months' pay at home.

"What is alarming is that members of specialized units
are resigning. It will have a negative effect to lose that experience—it takes at least a year to train them," Henrie
Boshoff, an Institute for Security Studies military analyst,
told the *Sunday Independent* newspaper in South Africa.[177]

WHO'S BEHIND ERINYS?

In Greek mythology, the Erinys are three goddesses, attendants of Hades and Persephone, who guarded the underworld. In Iraq, Erinys hold an $80 million contract, awarded by the occupation authorities in summer 2003, to provide security for Iraq's oil infrastructure. According to Pulitzer Prize–winning journalist Knut Royce of New York's *Newsday*, the company, like the fabled Erinys sisters, has a mysterious history.[178]

Soon after this security contract was issued, the company started recruiting many of its guards from the ranks of Ahmed Chalabi's former militia, the Free Iraqi Forces, raising allegations from other Iraqi officials that Chalabi was creating a private army. (Over one thousand men were recruited to the Free Iraqi Forces in the spring of 2003 and flown to camps in Hungary by the Pentagon where they were trained to fight against Saddam Hussein. Soon after the Americans occupied the country, the Iraqi National Congress disbanded the Free Iraqi Forces.)

Chalabi, scion of one of Iraq's most politically powerful and wealthy families until the monarchy was toppled in 1958, had been living in exile in London when the U.S. invaded Iraq. He was the chief architect of the Iraqi National Congress (INC), which received millions of dollars to help destabilize Saddam Hussein's regime before the invasion. Until his offices were raided in late May 2004, many Iraqis viewed Chalabi as America's hand-picked choice to rule Iraq.

The contract was technically awarded to Erinys Iraq, a security company newly formed after the invasion in a com-

plex venture bankrolled at its inception by Nour USA. Nour
was incorporated in the United States last May, according to
David Braus, the company's managing director. Nour's
founder was a Chalabi friend and business associate, Abul
Huda Farouki. Within days of the award last August, Nour
became a joint-venture partner with Erinys and the contract
was amended to include Nour.

An industry source familiar with some of the internal
affairs of both companies told Royce that Chalabi received a
$2 million fee for helping arrange the contract. Chalabi, in a
brief interview with *Newsday*, denied that claim, as did a
top company official. Chalabi also denied that he has had
anything to do with the security firm.

Yet the INC appears deeply connected to Erinys. For
example a founding partner and director of Erinys Iraq,
Faisal Daghistani, is the son of Tamara Daghistani, for years
one of Chalabi's most trusted confidants and a key player in
the creation of the INC.

In the 1980s Farouki's businesses received at least $12
million from a Chalabi-controlled bank in Washington, D.C.
The Jordanian government says that the bank was part of a
massive embezzlement scheme perpetrated by Chalabi on
the Petra bank he owned in Amman. When the bank collapsed in 1989, it cost the Jordanian government $200 mil-
lion to reimburse depositors and avert a collapse of the country's entire banking system.

Jordanian authorities have complained that much of the
funds they claim were siphoned off the Amman bank ended
up at Petra International. By May 1989, three months before
Jordan seized Petra Bank, the bankrupt Farouki companies
owed Petra International more than $12 million, court
records show.

LIVING IN FEAR

Financial scandals aside, these security groups seemed to be otherwise failing. With all their armed employees one would expect security on the ground to have improved. But Iraqis told a different story.

On my very first day in "liberated" Iraq, in December 2003, I met Ghazwan al Mukhtar, a retired Iraqi engineer who was active in the antisanctions movement for many years. He told me that not long ago he discovered a man in the street who was shot in the head and lay bleeding. Al Mukhtar took him to the police station and was infuriated when the police refused to investigate. "What has happened to us? We are no longer a civilized society but in a state of chaos. We are no longer safe in our own land."

Over the course of the next few months, I realized that security for ordinary Iraqis had completely disappeared. I discovered that all the cinemas were closed, the children's zoo and playgrounds were empty, the banks of the Tigris where musicians once performed on summer evenings had shut down. No, there was no ban on any of these activities; it was just fear of suicide bombs, American attacks, and street crime, the latter a hitherto unknown phenomenon under the dictator. The police didn't even bother to direct traffic in the streets; they would just watch the daily snarl-ups, while chatting away with each other and endlessly smoking cigarettes.

On my next trip to Baghdad, in April 2004, I visited the city morgue. I walked through the quiet hallways, their pink walls suffused with a meditative glow streaming in from the skylight. I met with Dr. Kais Hassan Salman, the director of statistics, who read off the numbers of people killed by bullet injuries. "January 2003, 13 cases; in February, 6; in March, 18 cases. In February [2004], 299; March, 413," he reported. The fatality rates were staggeringly different—roughly twenty-five times higher after the war than before it. Most of the dead were victims of common crime, others died as a result of political killings, and yet others were casualties of the American war.

INFILTRATION . . .

But are the police simply not doing their jobs? There is a growing suspicion that at least some of those who signed up for the police jobs may have other intentions. This issue came into sharp focus when Fern Holland, a Washington lawyer, and Robert Zangis, a computer software salesman from Virginia, were killed by Iraqi gunmen on a road near the holy city of Karbala on March 9, 2004. At first the incident raised some eyebrows when the American occupation authorities announced that the gunmen were disguised as policemen, but shock waves rolled over the military when they discovered that the five men really were members of the new Iraqi police force.[179]

Nor was this the first time that Iraqi police were discovered to have targeted the occupation authorities. Little more than a month earlier, soldiers from First Battalion, Twenty-second Infantry Regiment were observing a house in the village of Cadaseeya when they came under automatic weapons fire. The soldiers returned fire and threw a hand grenade at the attackers killing one of them who was later discovered to have been an active Iraqi police major.[180]

Nobody knows what motivated these men—hatred of the

occupation or support from clandestine underground forces—but it is becoming increasingly clear that the newly armed men have little loyalty, in no small part because they are so woefully underpaid. Police make $120 a month while soldier make almost half that, far less than what they could earn were they to work for private security companies or even as day laborers.

... OR DESERTION?

Perhaps no security project was so badly and publicly botched as the training of the First Battalion of the new Iraqi army. The U.S. occupation authorities fired all four hundred thousand soldiers in Saddam's army when they took control of Iraq in April 2004, drawing up plans to train forty thousand new soldiers in twenty-seven battalions by June 30, a number that they missed by a large margin.

By the day that the first group of 900 men was supposed to leave for their first assignment, 480 had abandoned their jobs because of low pay, inadequate training, faulty equipment, ethnic tensions, and other concerns, according to Australian Major Doug Cumming, chief instructor at the training academy in Kirkush, located about sixty miles northeast of Baghdad. Even worse, those that remained still had not learned how to march in formation and how to properly respond to radio calls.[181]

Surprisingly, the company hired to do the job, Vinnell Corporation, had been training the Saudi Arabian National Guard for twenty-five years. Yet a closer examination of their record suggests that maybe they weren't the best people for the job. First, the much vaunted Saudi Arabian National Guard has never proven itself in battle; so no conclusions can be drawn about how good or bad the training has been. Second, Vinnell's own facilities in Saudi Arabia had twice succumbed to attack.

Major General Paul Eaton, who was working with Vinnell at the Kirkush training camp, said he complained about the fact that the company was paying the soldiers far too little—seventy dollars a month. (By contrast the company was paid $48 million for the job.) Eaton also criticized the Vinnell's training methods, suggested training personnel were more akin to college professors than military instructors. "Soldiers need to train soldiers. You can't ask a civilian to do a soldier's job," he told the *Washington Post*. Instead of teaching strict discipline, the Vinnell trainers encouraged trainees to take time off, relax, and watch Sylvester Stallone and Jackie Chan movies.

One major source of tension in the First Battalion was the forced integration of ethnic Arabs and Kurds, traditional enemies. American planners thought that they could create a model for the country's diversity, so they picked 60 percent Arab Shiite, 20 percent Arab Sunni, 10 percent Kurdish Sunni, and 10 percent other. From the first day this was a nonstarter, because military training had to be translated from English to Arabic and then to Kurdish. Within the first few weeks one hundred Kurds quit after their tribal leaders objected to the battalion's ethnic mixture. The soldiers also complained that the uniforms looked funny and shrank in the wash. Plus, their weapons didn't work.[182]

The U.S. military reacted to the desertion problem by firing Vinnell and bringing in the Jordanian army to do the training. However the incidents have stirred uncomfortable memories for some military observers who remember that the American-backed mujahideen in Afghanistan recruited

IRAQ, INC.   127

among the Soviet-trained local soldiers and persuaded their
countrymen to hand over their weapons and abandon their
jobs. Could a similar situation be occurring in Iraq?

WE TRAIN PEOPLE TO PULL TRIGGERS

Despite Vinnell's failed contract, the company boasted a
long history of providing services to the U.S. military.
Vinnell Corporation, founded by the late A. S. Vinnell in
1931, began as a Los Angeles–based road-paving company.
Since then the company has handled a number of large
domestic as well as government projects. Vinnell was the
major contractor for U.S. military operations in Okinawa, it
overhauled Air Force planes in Guam in the early 1950s, and
sent men and equipment onto the battlefields of the Korean
War.[183] Now based in Fairfax, Virginia, the company has historically been controlled through a web of interlocking ownership by a partnership that included James Baker III and
Frank Carlucci, former U.S. secretaries of state and defense
under presidents George Bush Sr. and Ronald Reagan respec-
tively.

Perhaps the most important military contract Vinnell
landed was in 1975 when the Pentagon helped the company
win a bid to train the seventy-five-thousand-strong Saudi
Arabian National Guard, a military unit descended from
the Bedouin warriors who helped the Saud clan impose control on the peninsula early in the last century. An article in
Newsweek published at the time of Vinnell's winning the
contract described the company's first recruitment efforts
that were aided by "a one-eyed former U.S. Army colonel
named James D. Holland." In a cramped office in the Los
Angeles suburb of Alhambra, Holland assembled "a ragtag

army of Vietnam veterans for a paradoxical mission: to train Saudi Arabian troops to defend the very oil fields that Henry Kissinger recently warned the U.S. might one day have to invade."

"We are not mercenaries because we are not pulling triggers," a former U.S. Army officer told the magazine. "We train people to pull triggers." One of his colleagues wryly pointed out, "Maybe that makes us executive mercenaries."[184]

BLACKWATER: SECURITY GUARDS OR ACTIVE MILITARY?

On April Fool's Day 2004, Paul Bremer traveled from Baghdad to Mosul on a C-130 aircraft and then transferred to a Black Hawk helicopter that carried him to the Al-Rifah palace complex to meet with local representatives to discuss the Transitional Administrative Law.

John Burns and James Dao of *The New York Times* described the meeting thus:

> At a town meeting, where Bremer met with about 130 carefully vetted Iraqis, Blackwater guards maintained a heavy presence, standing along the walls facing the Iraqi guests with their rifles cradled.
>
> Perhaps the most striking thing about the entire visit was the metaphor it offered for the dilemma facing the American enterprise here: the fact that America's tribune for a democratic Iraq is so constrained by concerns for his personal security that he can only make his case to Iraqis inside a heavily-secured military complex, and before an audience of invited guests who, by definition, are already

proven friends of America and its purposes here.
Call it democracy in a flak jacket.[185]

Blackwater was founded in 1998 by former Navy Seals. At a remote six-thousand-acre training facility, hidden among horse farms and pine trees in North Carolina, the company has shooting ranges for high-powered weapons, buildings, and even a three-story-high model ship to practice attack missions. In 2002, the company won a five-year navy contract worth $35.7 million to train ten thousand navy personnel in seizing ships.[186]

At the end of March 2004, the company made headlines when four of their men, Wesley Batalona, Scott Helvenston, Michael Teague, and Jerko Zovko, were killed in an ambush as they were driving through the town of Fallujah.[187] Blackwater claims the convoy was providing security for Compass ESS, which has a contract to provide food services to the U.S. military, although no food trucks were described as even being close to the scene of the attack.[188]

Like Erinys, Blackwater hires South Africans and other experienced foreign fighters. "We scour the ends of the earth to find professionals," Blackwater President Gary Jackson told a reporter. In March 2004, Blackwater recruited sixty former Chilean commandos and other service members— many of whom had trained under the military government of Augusto Pinochet—and flew them to the company's training camp in North Carolina in preparation for jobs in Iraq, according to the *Guardian UK*.[189]

A few days later the *Washington Post* described Blackwater personnel taking part in a pitched battle in Najaf. "Before U.S. reinforcements could arrive, Blackwater sent in its own helicopters amid an intense firefight to resupply its commandos with ammunition and to ferry out a wounded Marine. The role of Blackwater...illuminates the gray zone between their formal role as bodyguards and the realities of operating in an active war zone," it reported.[190]

Do these private companies take part in active warfare? Could they even be involved in the planning of active military operations? It's hard to say without embedding an independent reporter inside the military planning meetings. However, the fact that they carry weapons in contravention of the terms of their contracts may be indicative of a greater role than that which they were officially assigned.

RIVAL ARMIES

Following the uprisings of April 2004, the occupation authorities have become painfully aware of the existence of shadowy armies and militias that are ready to pick up arms at a moment's notice, some of which may be tacitly supported by the local police or may even have overlapping memberships.

In the south, there are two rival Shiite militias, the Badr and the Mahdi. In Sadr City, the Mahdi army—named for a Shiite religious leader who, according to the prophecy, is to lead an apocalyptic battle—even has its own courts and prisons.[191] These men fought in the city of Karbala against American soldiers and supporters of Grand Ayatollah Ali al-Sistani immediately following the invasion and took control of Kut, Kufa, Najaf, Karbala, and other cities in April and May 2004. The Badr Organization, on the other hand, a militia commanded by Hassan al-Amari to serve the Supreme Council for the Islamic Revolution in Iraq, works directly with the police in Basra. Unconfirmed reports circulating in

April 2004 suggest that when the Mahdi took control of Najaf and the mujahideen beat back the Americans in Fallujah, the police simply took off their uniforms and joined them.

In the mountainous north there are the two Kurdish *peshmerga* armies—one loyal to Jalal Talibani and the other to Masoud Barzani. Although the *peshmerga* today work together, they have historically been rivals.

Rounding out the militias is the Iraqi National Accord, a group run by Ayad Allawi and backed by the Central Intelligence Agency during the invasion, which has since disbanded like the Free Iraqi Forces.[192] However, like the Free Iraqi Forces, they too can be said to have evolved rather than disbanded, because today the Iraqi National Accord runs the Interior Ministry, which controls many of the country's security forces, including the police. A spokesman for the Iraqi National Congress, Entifadh Qanbar, told *The New York Times* that "militias are very important in certain areas" and could serve as emergency forces.[193]

If the role of the Iraqi police appears a little unclear, the same is true of the highly paid American and British ex-soldiers. There is no doubt that these men and women's loyalty is to their occupation paymasters, but the big question is what are they really doing? Are they simply very well paid security guards or are they a paramilitary force? Even if they did not start out as a private militia, it appears that they maybe evolving into one.

WORLD'S LARGEST PRIVATE ARMY

In April 2004, rumors began to circulate that many of the private security contractors had started to band together, organizing what may be the largest private army in the world, with its own rescue teams and pooled, sensitive intelligence.

Nick Edmunds, Iraq coordinator for Hart (the group that hired the South African assassin killed in Kut), said, "There is absolutely a growing cooperation along unofficial lines. We try to give each other warnings about things we hear are about to happen."

"There is no formal arrangement for intelligence-sharing," Colonel Jill Morgenthaler, a spokeswoman for the occupation authorities in Baghdad, wrote in an email response to questions from the *Washington Post*. "However, ad hoc relationships are in place so that contractors can learn of dangerous areas or situations."[194] From the point of view of the contractors, this was a logical step. Many of them felt that the military was not very cooperative in providing sensitive information and the only way they could protect themselves was to create their own intelligence apparatus. But given that not all of these contractors have the shiniest of reputations, one could question whether this sharing of information might lead to revenge killings or even mistaken attacks on innocent people.

The sharing of resources has another important consequence: the blurring of these groups in the public eye. As far as the Iraqi public is concerned, the private military contractors—the men with guns who do not wear military uniforms—are CIA, and therefore legitimate targets. We were told repeatedly that the Baghdad hotel, officially a Dyncorp residence for police trainers, was a CIA base. In the eyes of the angry young man on Saddoun Street, the difference was unimportant—the hotel was housing the equivalent of the SS of Nazi Germany, of the Mukhabarat of Saddam's Iraq.

This conflation is behind the resistance's strategy of targeting security contract workers. For example, the four Italian hostages who made grisly headlines in April 2004 when one of them was executed on videotape were private security contractors. Fabrizio Quattrocchi, Maurizio Agliana, and Umberto Cupertino worked for a Nevada-based security firm called DTS. The fourth man, Salvatore Stefio, was president of a private security company called Presidium. (Quattrocchi was videotaped being killed with a shot to the head.)[195]

At least one security company, Bidepa, from Romania, which commanded a staff of eight working under a three-month contract as bodyguards for members of Iraq's puppet government, pulled out of Iraq after one of its workers was killed and another injured in an ambush near Baghdad in April 2004, according to its director Dumitru Nicolae.[196]

Maybe these attacks were unintentional, but I got the distinct impression that private security contractors are among the top three targets, the other two being soldiers and Iraqi politicians or collaborators.

CONTROVERSIAL COMMANDO

Weeks after the ambushes of the Europeans, the army had a more formal system in place for information sharing with contractors, but to the surprise of even the security companies themselves, the task of coordinating top-secret intelligence was handed over to yet another private company, rather than a military authority. And to the anger of many, the task was given to a company run by a man with the dodgiest of reputations: Aegis Defence Services, headed by Lieutenant Colonel Tim Spicer, a former officer with the

Scots Guard, an elite regiment of the British military, who has been investigated for illegally smuggling arms and planning military offensives to support mining, oil, and gas operations around the world.

The $293 million contract, awarded on May 25, 2004, was a "cost-plus" contract that included providing seventy-five close protection teams, comprised of eight men each, for the high-level staff of companies overseeing the oil and gas fields and electricity and water services in Iraq.

Major Gary Tallman, a spokesperson for the U.S. Army, explained to me that the contract was to create an "integrator" or coordination hub for the security operation for every single reconstruction contractor and subcontractor. "Their job is to disseminate information and provide guidance and coordination throughout the four regions of Iraq."[197]

Rumors of lucrative new jobs with Spicer had been circulating for a couple of months. In late March, Britain's Lieutenant Colonel Alan Browne, who is in charge of finding jobs for members of the Royal Signals Regiment in Blandford Camp, Dorset, posted ads offering Aegis positions in Iraq for qualified radio technicians. The posted salary of $110,000 a year is three times higher than most other jobs offered at the regimental resettlement office. The contract also provides a generous one hundred days of vacation per year.

"Our men can repair anything from a radio to a satellite phone, but the pay here in the U.K. is just twenty-five thousand pounds [forty-six thousand dollars]," Browne told me. "I posted the job to the guys and now it's up to them to go get the jobs."

Also, in late March, jobs were posted at the Adjutant General's Corps in Worthy Down, Winchester, for clerks to maintain "clerical and administrative support for a head-quarters-type environment similar to a military brigade/divisional headquarters with many of the same divisions of responsibility." Salaries offered for candidates with senior-noncommissioned-officer qualifications were $129,000, and candidates with junior-noncommissioned-officer qualifications could earn $110,000.[198]

Tallman says that seven companies bid for the coordination contract. According to confidential sources, the bidders included Dyncorp; Military Professionals Resources Incorporated (MPRI), one of the companies training the Iraqi army; and a joint venture comprising Control Risks Group, Erinys, and Olive Security, three of the largest providers of private security in Iraq. The losing bidders were not happy. In late June 2004, Dyncorp filed a protest at the General Accouting Office against the contract with Spicer.[199]

But Aegis's competitors were not the only ones that deemed them unfit for the job. Analyst Peter Singer, author of Corporate Warriors: The Rise of the Privatized Military Industry and a fellow at the Brookings Institution, a liberal Washington, D.C.–based think tank, argues that Aegis should never have gotten the contract.

> The contract is a case study in what not to do.... To begin with, a core problem of the military outsourcing experience has been the lack of coordination, oversight and management from the government side. So outsourcing that very problem to another private company has a logic that would do only Kafka proud. In addition, it moves these companies further outside the bounds of public oversight.
>
> The usual mechanisms that increase efficiency

in contracting—like choosing, rewarding and pun-
ishing firms based on their experience and reputa-
tion—have again been short-circuited. One would
think such a major contract would go to a company
that has a long operating history, or experience in
such roles, or other major activities on the ground
in Iraq. Instead, Aegis has been in existence for little more than a year, has worked primarily on
antipiracy efforts rather than security coordination,
and has never before had a major contract in Iraq.[200]

But not everyone agrees with this assessment of Spicer's
work. In Sierra Leone, Spicer's efforts have been hailed by
the private military industry as the "work of angels." In
1998, Spicer's firm, Sandline International, a private military company that employed top ranking ex-military personal before shutting down operations in April 2004, was contracted to sell thirty tons of arms to the forces of Ahmad
Tejan Kabbah, the former leader of Sierra Leone, in contravention of a UN arms embargo but in apparent cooperation
with Craig Murray, a junior staffer at the British Foreign
Office. Doug Brooks, president of International Peace
Operations Association (IPOA), a nonprofit advocacy group
for private military companies including Sandline, says the
company's assistance in Sierra Leone saved the lives of thousands of civilians. "Sandline was remarkably effective,"
Brooks said. "Their goal of restoring the democratically
elected government was achieved. They maintained a low
profile but played a critical role in the success."[201]
Nonetheless, Sandline's Sierra Leone project provoked a
furor and multiple government investigations in Britain
when it was discovered that the contract violated the United

Nations embargo on providing arms to either side in the military conflict. Spicer maintains that he was unaware that the scheme was illegal and the government eventually agreed to draw up new rules on arms trafficking and the conduct of private military companies in Britain.[202]

Spicer's work in Papua New Guinea, another public relations fiasco, failed even in military terms. The eastern half of the South Pacific island of New Guinea, Papua New Guinea (PNG), was a British and German colony and then an Australian protectorate until 1975. That year, both PNG and the outlying island of Bougainville, some five hundred miles northeast of the capital, Port Moresby, declared independence. PNG quickly took over Bougainville, where an Australian company, CRA (now part of Rio Tinto, the world's largest mining company), had begun to mine copper in 1972.

In 1989, local landowners shut down the Bougainville copper mine to protest the environmental destruction it caused and to demand independence. In February 1997, the PNG government, which had received about 44 percent of its revenue from the mine, paid Sandline International $36 million to rout the Bougainvilleans.

The very next month, PNG Prime Minister Julius Chan sacked the military commander, Brigadier General Jerry Singarok, for denouncing the contract with Sandline and arguing that the money would be better spent on his own troops, who were desperately underpaid and ill-equipped. Riots ensued after soldiers loyal to Singarok led protests drawing more than two thousand civilians. The soldiers arrested and deported a number of the Sandline contractors.

Less than a month later, dressed in crumpled jeans, Spicer was led into a Papua New Guinea court. His suitcase, bulging with four hundred thousand dollars in cash, was produced as evidence of his contract with the disgraced government. At the hearings, Spicer revealed that one aspect of the project (code-named "Operation Oyster") was to wage a psychological campaign against the Bougainvilleans with the help of Russian-style attack helicopters. Spicer's lawyers worked overtime to get the charges reduced and eventually dismissed, but Chan was forced to resign from his job.[203]

CACI AND TITAN

Apart from doing security-guard duty supporting military offensives, private contractors have also landed plum jobs for traditional intelligence work, such as interrogation. Easily the most well known of these contracts were carried out in the now infamous torture chambers of Abu Ghraib.

The background to these contracts is similar to almost every other outsourcing venture in the military. That is, contracts were offered as an official effort to reduce workforce numbers and save money, according to David Isenberg, an analyst who follows private military companies for the British American Security Information Council.[204] In the past, interrogators would typically be trained at intelligence schools, located at posts such as the army's interrogation school at Fort Huachuca in southern Arizona. According to unconfirmed reports in *WorldNet* magazine, the military slashed pay for instructors by 50 percent in January 2002, causing many of them to quit.[205]

However, new job opportunities materialized quickly, in the opening of American-run prisons holding Al Qaeda suspects in Afghanistan and at Guantánamo Bay, and eventually, in Iraqi prisons holding former Ba'athists. Instead of reinvesting in military training, the Pentagon opted to hire interrogators and translators from private companies.

Two companies stepped up to the plate. The first, CACI International from Arlington, Virginia (referred to as "Khaki" in military circles), had previously gone by the name California Analysis Center Incorporated. Formed in the sixties by Harry Markowitz (a Nobel Prize winner for economics in 1990 for his research on stock portfolio diversification), CACI won its first federal contracts for custom-written computer languages that could be used to build battlefield simulation programs.[206]

CACI, which employs roughly sixty-three hundred people, had long pursued an aggressive, expansionist business strategy, focused on acquiring weaker companies and pumping up its business with the federal government through contracts for personnel support at the Kelly Air Force Base in Texas and the McClellan Air Force Base in California.[207] Its profits doubled between 2001 and 2003, skyrocketing from $22 million (on total revenues of $557 million) to $44 million (on revenues of $843 million).[208]

The company's management and board boasted a roster of former soldiers and spies, including board members Michael Bayer, former vice chairman of the Pentagon's Business Board, and advisor to the air force, army, U.S. Naval War College, and Sandia National Laboratory; Barbara McNamara, ex-deputy director of the National Security Agency; Arthur Money, former assistant secretary of defense; and Larry Welch, an ex-air force general who served on the joint chiefs of staff during the first Bush administration.[209]

With the new contracts, CACI immediately started soliciting on its Web site for interrogators to be dispatched to Afghanistan, Iraq, and Kosovo. Would-be interrogators were told that they would have to be comfortable working under "moderate supervision," providing "intelligence support for interviewing local nationals, and determining there [sic] threat to coalition forces." Further, propective employees were required to be able to work with interpreters to gather intelligence information from multiple sources. According to CACI's site, the jobs required "a Top Secret Clearance (TS) that is current and U.S. citizenship," and candidates must "have at least two years' experience as a military policeman or similar type of law enforcement/intelligence agency [experience,] whereby the individual utilized interviewing techniques."[210] One CACI employee, Joe Ryan, kept an online blog about his work at Abu Ghraib. The blog was hosted on the Web site of KSTP-AM, a St. Paul, Minnesota radio station, but the journal was quickly removed from the Internet once the prison scandal became public. In an entry dated April 21, 2004, Ryan described the praise he and his coworkers received after turning in an interrogation analysis. "The command was thrilled and once again the CACI folks have set a high standard for the younger soldiers to follow," he wrote.[211]

The second company competing for its share of the clandestine interrogation business is Titan Corporation of San Diego, California, a twenty-three-year-old company with a staff of nearly twelve thousand and revenues of about $2 billion a year. Titan made its money selling information and communication services to military and spy agencies. Under one of its contracts Titan sells communication hardware systems to the U.S. military. It currently services a $3 billion contract in a joint venture with five other companies to provide radios, signal repeaters, and related communications equipment to the Secret Service, the Drug Enforcement

Administration, and the Federal Bureau of Investigation to help them communicate with one another through a common standard called Project 25.[212]

Titan also builds a modified Humvee called the Prophet that allows its driver to locate and target people in the surrounding area who are using electronic communication ranging from unencrypted push-to-talk radios to cell phones. The vehicle is equipped with a collapsible seven-meter antenna mast that can go up or down in ninety seconds and a special seat for a translator. The Prophet was first tested in Afghanistan and newer versions allow multiple vehicles to act in concert to attack targets.[213]

In addition, Titan has a $54.8 million contract to provide support to the Airborne Warning and Control System (AWACS) spy planes,[214] as well as an $18 million contract to design war games for the U.S. Navy's Pacific Fleet. Under the latter contract, Titan designs over 150 war games each year to support a training curricula and predeployment work-up training for several arms of the military.[215]

In 2003, Titan earned $112.1 million for translation services to the U.S. military around the world. The company got into this business in 1999, aggressively recruiting translators in Arabic, Aramaic, Dari, Farsi, Georgian, Kurdish, Pashto, Tajik, Ughyur, Urdu, and Uzbek by faxing community groups and visiting job fairs and language clubs. A toll-free number (1-800-899-6200) and email addresses for Titan employees Basir Kakar and Chiman Zebari have appeared on numerous discussion groups.[216]

A Titan ad posted to Afghan groups read as follows:

> This unique employment opportunity affords you the chance to simultaneously assist Afghanistan

and the United States in forging a new and promising future for the Afghan people and to bolster global security.... As a Titan Systems Corporation contractor linguist, you will be called upon to support critical missions such as interpreting during interviews, translating key documents of interest, and providing the U.S. Government with an understanding of the culture that only a native can provide.

To qualify as a Titan Systems linguist you must be a U.S. citizen, pass a language test, and be subject to a U.S. government background investigation.... Some work environments and conditions are harsh, but the rewards are great. If you or someone you know is interested in a meaningful job that offers great pay, benefits and the chance to make a positive impact in the war on terrorism, please contact us.[217]

The jobs required a willingness to travel on short notice and offered a salary of as much as $108,000 a year, most of that tax-free.[218]

A couple of months before the invasion of Iraq, similar notices were faxed and mailed to Kurdish community organizations in Nashville, Dallas, and San Diego—the three cities in the United States with the largest Kurdish populations.

In December 2002, the Associated Press quoted two brothers in Nashville—Diyar Mustafa, an apartment maintenance worker, and his brother, Idris, a school district custodian—who traveled to Washington for the week-long job interview. Both of them had previously been tortured in

Saddam's Iraq, making them questionable recruits from a human rights point of view, because of the possibility of their wanting to exact revenge.[219]

Emad Mikha, a Chaldean from Basra, living in the United States, was another Titan recruit. Until Mikha was hired by Titan in November 2003 as a civilian translator for the army based in Baqubah, Iraq, he managed the meat department at a supermarket in Pontiac, Michigan. Mikha was killed in the first week of April, a week that saw the largest antioccupation uprisings across the country to date.

Like many other contractors in Iraq, Titan workers often carried weapons (technically illegal under United States military law) and traveled with the troops, making them easy targets for the underground resistance, which viewed them as traitors.[220] Titan's translators have also been accused of working for the other side. Ahmed Fathy Mehalba, a taxi driver from Boston, was one of seventy Titan translators hired to aid interrogations in Guantánamo Bay, Cuba. He was arrested in September 2003 after returning from his native Egypt with what authorities claimed was classified information from the Cuban base. Mehalba had previously failed army interrogation school in Fort Huachuca, Arizona and received a medical discharge from the army in May 2001. A girlfriend he met there was dishonorably discharged after allegedly being caught with a stolen laptop containing classified information. According to the affidavit, Mehalba said he did not know how the information, some of it marked secret, got on the disc. He told the FBI interrogators that he got the CD from an uncle who had worked in military intelligence in Egypt but had long since retired.[221]

OTHER SPOOKS

Who else is working on these private intelligence jobs in Iraq? Well, certainly former CIA officers, although it is not clear if they are independent contractors or working through companies. The Associated Press quotes former CIA agents, called "green badgers" because of the color of their I.D.s, who claim that as contractors they can earn triple their government salaries—grossing as much as $150,000 annually.[222]

Certainly there are many intelligence contractors whose names have only become public once they were killed or disappeared. Kirk von Ackermann of Moss Beach, California, was one such contractor; he disappeared on October 9, 2003. His car was found abandoned between the cities of Tikrit and Kirkuk. Found inside the vehicle were his satellite phone, a laptop computer, and a briefcase containing around forty thousand dollars, suggesting that he had not been the victim of a robbery.

His immediate employer was Ultra Services, a company based in Istanbul that furnishes supplies and logistics help for U.S. Army bases in Iraq. A former U.S. Air Force captain who worked for Impact Intelligence, he had been a member of a Pentagon group that provided intelligence on terrorism, espionage, information warfare, and other threats. Previously he had served as deputy director of intelligence for NATO operations in Bosnia.[223]

Finally there are the computer technology surveillance and database programmers needed to support intelligence work. One such person was Michael Pouliot, executive vice president and cofounder of San Diego-based Tapestry Solutions, a company specializing in military modeling and

simulation training tools. Pouliot was in Kuwait to install
software that would allow the military to coordinate its
operations, according to a company statement.[224] Two
months before the invasion of Iraq, just north of Kuwait
City, he was killed. For contractors big and small, operating
in Iraq is a matter of taking one's life into one's own hands.

ACCOUNTING TROUBLES AND BRIBERY INVESTIGATIONS

Titan's dealings around the world have come under scrutiny,
and Iraq is no exception. In March 2004, the Pentagon's
Defense Contract Audit Agency (DCAA) discovered "deficiencies in the labor accounting controls" of Titan in Iraq,
which prompted them to penalize the company. William
Reed, DCAA director, said in an interview, "In layman's language it basically says 'You submit a bill to us and we are
only going to pay 90 percent of it until you fix these labor
accounting deficiencies.'"

DCAA said Titan had inadequate systems for documenting its billing of the Pentagon for labor costs and for tracking the work of non-American consultants. The agency
threatened to withhold as much as $4.9 million in payments
until the company fixed accounting deficiencies uncovered
by the audit.

"Titan has already taken the corrective actions to comply
with the government's concerns. We are continuing to work
with the government as they review our process related to
this difficult operational environment in Iraq," Titan
spokesman Wil Williams told reporters in an emailed statement at the time.[225]

According to my sources, Titan also is currently being
investigated for bribing officials in Indonesia, Ivory Coast,

Nigeria, Saudi Arabia, and Zimbabwe.[226] The *Wall Street Journal* has also suggested that the company is being investigated in Bangladesh and the Philippines.

The criminal investigation was triggered when Lockheed Martin, a Bethesda, Maryland–based military contractor, made an offer to buy the company for $1.8 billion. Because Lockheed is the biggest contractor to the Pentagon, the government performed a routine antimonopoly check, which uncovered the bribery scandals.[227]

This, in turn, led the Justice Department and the SEC to begin separate investigations into "allegations relating to certain payments and provisions of items of value to foreign officials, which, if true, raise questions as to whether Titan has violated the Foreign Corrupt Practices Act," Titan Chief Executive Officer Gene Ray wrote in a March 8 letter to customers.[228]

"These are allegations; not evidence of wrongdoing," Williams told reporters. But Lockheed itself is no angel in these matters; in 1995 the company pleaded guilty and paid a $24.8 million fine for conspiring to bribe an Egyptian politician for help in securing a contract for three C-130H cargo jets.[229]

According to *Wall Street Journal* sources, most of Titan's contracts appeared to be for military-radio systems. Sam Dailey, a marketing manager at Datron World Communications, the Titan unit that makes military-radio systems, was interviewed about payments to such representatives as part of the internal inquiry, and one of his associates was suspended without pay as a result of the investigation.[230]

Shane Harris, technology editor of *Government Executive* magazine in Washington, DC, told me that Titan has also been heavily criticized for a contract to provide mental health services to military service members because of apparent conflict of interest, as described below, in designing the contract that they would eventually win. In addition, Titan has no prior experience in the field, Harris said.[331]

In August 2003, the General Services Administration (GSA), on behalf of the Defense Department, chose Titan and a company called Ceridian to provide Employee Assistance Program (EAP) services for the military as part of the supplemental appropriations for ongoing operations in Iraq. According to a recent article by Harris, Titan secured the contract through questionable conduct on the part of its partner, Ceridian:

> A draft copy of the request for proposals for this work, detailing the specific requirements contractors must meet, appears to have been at least partially written by a Ceridian employee. The file properties of the Microsoft Word electronic document, obtained by Government Executive, list as the author a person whose name matches that of a senior official in Ceridian's public sector division....
>
> Other details in the electronic document indicate it was sent via e-mail to at least one other Ceridian employee with a subject line stating it was a draft request for proposals. But the document begins with a formal heading indicating it is being issued by GSA's Federal Technology Service (FTS), a fee-for-service unit that runs information technology procurements on behalf of other agencies. The

document also features an order numbering system routinely used by GSA when putting work up for bid.[232]

TORTURE AT ABU GHRAIB

Both Titan and CACI were heavily implicated in the Abu Ghraib torture scandals in a fifty-three-page classified internal army report written by Major General Antonio Taguba, in which the actions of four civilian contractors—Steven Stephanowicz, John Israel, Torin Nelson, and Adel Nakhla—are described. All four contractors were assigned to work with the 205th Military Intelligence Brigade, a unit normally stationed in Germany and Italy in support of V Corps, under the command of Colonel Thomas Pappas.

According to the army report, Stephanowicz, a CACI interrogator, "made a false statement to the investigation team regarding the locations of his interrogations, the activities during his interrogations, and his knowledge of abuses." Further, investigators found Stephanowicz encouraged military police to terrorize inmates, and "clearly knew his instructions equated to physical abuse." Israel, a subcontractor to Titan, apparently misled investigators, denying that he witnessed any misconduct. The report says that Israel should not even have been there because he "did not have a security clearance." Nakhla was questioned about the treatment of several detainees accused of rape and was quoted as saying that two army sergeants made the prisoners, who were naked, do "strange exercises" and then "started to stack them on top of each other" after handcuffing them and shackling their legs. One civilian was accused of raping a juvenile Iraqi inmate but the name of the civilian was not revealed in the report. "In general, U.S. civilian contract personnel [Titan Corporation, CACI, etc.], third-country nationals, and local contractors do not appear to be properly supervised within the detention facility at Abu Ghraib," military investigators concluded.[233]

(The Bush administration claimed that the torture was limited to a few bad soldiers, but, at the time of writing, new reports are being uncovered every day that suggested otherwise. One Red Cross report revealed their investigators had found naked prisoners covering themselves with packages from ready-to-eat military rations, and being subjected to "deliberate physical violence and verbal abuse." Prisoners were found to be incoherent, anxious, and even suicidal, with abnormal symptoms "provoked by the interrogation period and methods." The document stated that prison authorities "could not explain" the lack of clothing for prisoners and "could not provide clarification" about other mistreatment of prisoners.)[234]

In subsequent investigations, it has emerged that almost all of the twenty-nine contract interrogators at Abu Ghraib were CACI employees, had a college education, and held a secret or top-secret clearance. Eleven of the twenty-nine employees served in the military previously, others in police forces. Kevin Bloodworth, an air force veteran from Great Falls, Montana, was nicknamed Blood, while Timothy Duggan, an interrogator from Pataskala, Ohio, was called Big Dog. Kenneth Powell, whose job it was to screen prisoners at Abu Ghraib, according to the documents, worked for the Mobile, Alabama police force.[235]

Torin Nelson, who worked at the Guantánamo Bay prison for a year with the Utah National Guard and then took a private sector job with CACI, spoke out against his former employer saying, "As far as control from supervisors, well, let me just say that it was also minimal. When it came to interrogation operations, we were pretty much free to operate how we wanted."[236] Earlier, the *Guardian UK* reported Nelson's account of his first encounter with CACI: "I was interviewed in September 2003 in a very short telephone conversation, which was more like a sales pitch of how great the company was, than a typical interview for a professional job. I never met anyone from CACI until I landed in Fort Bliss [an army induction center in Texas], and then it was some other new hires," said the former interrogator[237]

One of Nelson's colleagues at CACI was Stephanowicz, who described an interrogation tool that he called a "sleep meal management program," in which prisoners were allowed no more than four hours of sleep in a twenty-four-hour period, in a regime that usually lasted seventy-two hours.[238]

The Titan translators had even less qualifications or security clearances. John Israel, a Christian Iraqi American from Santa Clarita, California, was hired by SOS Interpreting to work as a subcontractor to Titan. He says he arrived in Iraq on October 14 and served as a translator for military intelligence. Like him, nearly all of the fifteen Titan or SOS translators working at Abu Ghraib prison were foreign-born Americans, and only one held a security clearance.

Most of his colleagues had previously worked in very ordinary jobs: Khalid Oman, who was born in Saudi Arabia, was a hotel manager in Kalamazoo, Michigan, before leaving for Iraq to work as a translator for Titan at Abu Ghraib; Bakeer Naseef, a Jordanian American, who worked as a security guard at the reception desk of a technology company in

Austin, Texas, was the only one to hold a "secret" clearance; Adel Nakhla, an Egyptian American, worked for Abacus Enterprises, a computer networking company, for seventeen months before leaving his townhouse in Gaithersburg, Maryland to go to work for Titan in Iraq.[239] Subsequently Nakhla was one of the guards shown in the infamous Abu Ghraib photos. Standing over several naked prisoners stacked in a pile, he is reaching down, his hand shown on or near a prisoner's neck. Nakhla, a big, burly man, claims he was not forceful. "I held the detainee's foot. Not in any powerful way."[240]

INVESTIGATE THE INTERROGATORS

Staff Sergeant Ivan "Chip" Frederick is one of the soldiers named in the Taguba report currently facing a court martial. His uncle, William Lawson, told me that his nephew said the private interrogators were partially responsible for the abuses. "He tried to complain and he was told by superior officers to follow instructions from civilian contract workers interrogating the Iraqi prisoners. They said 'Go back down there. Do what the civilian contractors tell you to do and don't interfere with them and loosen these soldiers up for interrogation.'"

Lawson demanded that the company employees should be investigated and prosecuted if necessary. "I've spent twenty-three years in the military including time in Vietnam. I love this country, but I will not allow my nephew to be used as a scapegoat," he said in a phone interview from his home in Newburg, West Virginia.[241]

In a canned statement issued on May 5, 2004, CACI CEO Jack London said, "CACI does not condone or tolerate or endorse in any fashion any illegal, inappropriate behavior on the part of any of its employees in any circumstance at any time anywhere. If, regrettably, any CACI employee was involved in any way at any time in any of the alleged behavior that occurred in Iraq and has been reported in the media and elsewhere, for those employees I will certainly personally take immediate, appropriate action."[242]

But legal experts say that civilians working for the military are subject to neither Iraqi nor military justice. One reason is because in June 2003, Bremer granted broad immunity to civilian contractors and their employees. They were, he wrote, generally not subject to criminal and civil actions in the Iraqi legal system, including arrest and detention.

There have been some recent, although relatively untested, laws that might fill the legal vacuum. A 1994 law makes torture committed by Americans outside the United States a crime. The law defines torture as the infliction of severe physical or mental pain or suffering, but the law only applies if they government labels their actions as "torture."

A 1996 law—the *Military Extraterritorial Jurisdiction Act* of 1996—allows people "employed by or accompanying the armed forces outside the United States" to be prosecuted in U.S. courts for violations of some provisions of the Geneva Conventions, including those prohibiting torture, "outrages upon personal dignity," and "humiliating and degrading treatment." Under this law, citizens or residents of the host nations are not covered, but Americans and other foreign nationals are. The law provides for long prison sentences, and capital punishment is available in cases involving the victim's death.

The Bush administration has used this law as a reason to withhold the protections of the Geneva Conventions from detainees at Guantánamo Bay. But the administration has said that the conventions do apply to detainees in Iraq. However, only contractors employed by the Pentagon may be prosecuted under the 1996 Act. Contractors hired by other agencies—the CIA or the Department of Interior—are not covered.[243]

SMOKEY THE BEAR CONTRACT

The interrogators at Abu Ghraib were working, not under a military contract, but one from the Department of the Interior's National Business Center at Fort Huachuca in Sierra Vista, Arizona, seventy miles southeast of Tucson. The arrangement was a result of federal efforts in the 1990s to "streamline and reduce duplication," by having agencies with particular skill at administrative functions, such as payroll or contracting, handle those jobs for other agencies.

In 2001, the Interior Department contracting office awarded a "blanket purchase agreement" to a company called Premier Technology Group (PTG) for services to be provided to the army. The agreement allowed the government to buy services from PTG without going through a new round of competitive bidding for each new job. After 2001, the department approved eighty-one "delivery orders" under the Premier Technology–CACI contract, including eleven for services in Iraq. In 2003, CACI acquired Premier Technology, allowing the government to buy services from them without inviting outside bids. Most of the services relate to information technology, but at least two did not— one for $19.9 million covering "interrogation support" and another for $21.8 million labeled "human intelligence support."

Critics ridiculed the arrangement. "You're placing a military interrogation task under Smokey the Bear. You can't have good oversight," says Peter Singer of the Brookings Institution.[244] And a government investigation by the GAO shows that the Pentagon has a backlog of nearly two hundred thousand people working for CACI and other contractors still awaiting security clearances. The average time required to grant a security clearance for a contract employee now exceeds one year. Plus there remains a backlog of sixty-one thousand reinvestigations for renewals that must be done every five years.

In congressional testimony in October 2003, Charles Abell, principal deputy under the secretary of defense for personnel, acknowledged that some contract employees were being sent to Iraq before they had received their security clearances because of "our rush to meet the requirements, the mere numerical requirements."[245]

CONCLUSION

In the previous chapter, I stressed that Iraqis' perception that contractors have fixed nothing in Iraq had effectively nullified any good work that the reconstruction might have accomplished. Similarly, the presence of the vast army of private security has led to greater distrust and to anger. The occupation is caught in a Catch-22 situation—either withdraw the private security people and get killed, or beef them up to take the place of soldiers and inflame the anger of the local population. In the latter event, the incident in Fallujah could well be repeated.

And, then of course, the presence of these private security forces prompts a more basic question: Who are these peo-

ple we have hired? If at least some of them were arms smug-
glers, notorious killers, or torturers in the past, could we be
creating a monster? The spy agencies have long used private
contractors to act as middlemen to ensure "plausible denia-
bility," especially during the Cold War, when they wanted to
ship covert military supplies to the anticommunist opposition in locales as far flung as Afghanistan and Nicaragua.
The men they hired in the past included a number of ex-
Nazis such as Ernst Werner Glatt and Gerhard Mertens who
helped provide arms to Saddam Hussein and the Afghan
mujahideen.[246]

The use of private companies to provide security guards
and interrogators has turned this occasional phenomenon
into an industry. The argument that this saves money
proves spurious, as I suggest in chapter one, since we pay
these contractors much more than state employees. (Ironical
especially since many of the contractors were trained by
United States military or intelligence schools in the first
place.) Were they working just occasionally, the cost-effi-
ciency argument might hold up, but in the case of Iraq where
employment is year-round, it fails. But the contracts represent more than just a waste of money. More importantly, the
public has no control or oversight of these groups because
the budgets on the government side are often clandestine
and the companies, for their part, certainly don't plan to
reveal any of their secrets for "proprietary business" reasons. The fact that these companies have hired staff who
failed to make the government grade, have a bad human
rights record, or simply might have a motive for revenge,
makes this phenomenon even scarier.

At the end of April 2004, the bloodiest month to date for
the occupation, five Democratic senators finally woke up to

what was happening in Iraq and asked the GAO to investigate the use and activities of private military contractors in Iraq.

The six-page letter, signed by Senators Christopher Dodd of Connecticut, Jack Reed of Rhode Island, Patrick Leahy of Vermont, Jon Corzine of New Jersey, and Russell Feingold of Wisconsin poses multiple questions on thirty-five subjects involving the contractors, ranging from who they are and how many have been injured or killed so far, to an explanation of government costs and accountability. The senators asked the auditors at the GAO the following: "In what ways might it endanger the lives of United States servicemen and women to be operating or cooperating with these firms or to be located in areas where PMFs [private military firms] are carrying out their own operations?"[247]

The senators also asked the GAO to address the private contractors' liabilities, including whether they are subject to the Uniform Code of Military Justice, and who has jurisdiction to punish them if they commit crimes. The administration's response has been weak at best, and at worse it signals consent to a system of grave impunity.

CHAPTER FOUR

Shadow Government

If military logisticians, reconstruction companies, and security/intelligence contractors were enjoying a boon from the war in Iraq, their fortunes were incidental to the prize claimed by contractors in statecraft and the privatization of the Iraqi economy. After all, war and its exigencies were only the means to regime change, the thing itself.

The American public was lead to believe that some permutation or combination of the Pentagon, the CIA, the State Department, and the White House call the shots in Iraq. While this is generally true, these bureaucrats have found the day-to-day operation of Iraq's government and politics rather bewildering. Put simply, they had no idea how to go about the process of "nation building." Nor did they get much help from the Iraqi Governing Council that they had appointed. The council is made up of politically ambitious cons and exiles with little bureaucratic experience, and it is rife with members who spent most of their time trying to cash in on their position of influence. It was widely rumored that the reason the council sessions were never televised was because the council chambers were usually near empty as the members jet-set to and from reconstruction conferences around the world.

So, in February 2003, the occupation planners turned to a private company, contracting Science Applications International Corporation (SAIC) of San Diego, California, to set up the Iraqi Reconstruction and Development Council (IRDC) in Arlington, Virginia, effectively a shadow "government in exile" of Iraqi Americans who would plan the running of the country in the event that Saddam Hussein was ousted.[248]

STEALTH COMPANY

What is SAIC? SAIC is one of the top ten Pentagon contractors,[249] one of the top five CIA contractors, and reportedly, the number one National Security Agency (NSA) contractor.[250] In 2003, the virtually unknown company generated $5.9 billion in revenue and ranked number 289 on the Fortune 500 list of the largest U.S. companies.[251] SAIC's biggest source of income is surveillance services for the United States spy agencies; some five thousand of its employees (or one in eight) have security clearances.[252]

"We are a stealth company," Keith Nightingale, a former army special operations officer, told the San Francisco–based magazine *Business 2.0*. "We're everywhere, but almost never seen." Founded in 1969 by physicist J. Robert Beyster, SAIC is an employee-owned, decentralized company. Beyster was formerly a nuclear scientist with the Los Alamos National Laboratory and holds one of the highest top-secret clearances of any civilian in the country. SAIC made a fortune during the dot-com boom by buying Network Solutions, the Web domain name keeper, for $4.5

million in 1996 and selling it for $3.1 billion before the bubble burst.[253]

SAIC has won dozens of government contracts. It trains air marshals for the Federal Aviation Administration, works with Bechtel to run the proposed Yucca Mountain nuclear waste dump in Nevada on Western Shoshone traditional lands (despite major protests from the Native Americans), and has a contract to destroy old chemical weapons at Aberdeen Proving Ground. The National Cancer Institute contracts SAIC to help run its research facility in Frederick, Maryland, the Transportation Security Administration asked it to dispose of scissors and pocket knives confiscated from air travelers, and SAIC's unmanned Vigilante helicopters, equipped with Raytheon's low-cost, precision-kill rockets, are soon to undergo testing by the army.[254]

Today two of SAIC's most valuable products are TeraText and Latent Semantic Indexing (LSI), data-mining programs that are used by intelligence agencies (such as the NSA) to sift the immense volumes of data they now collect by monitoring phone calls, faxes, e-mails, and other types of electronic communications. TeraText can process two billion documents every four seconds by identifying patterns and connections between names, terms, and ideas. For example, a CIA analyst might type in a request for all documents mentioning the name "Paris," the word "sleeper," and the term "planc" (a possible code for a suicide bombing attack), organizing the search by language and time of day to instantly retrieve all places in which the terms appeared in, say, a single sentence. LSI uses artificial intelligence that allows it to make judgments from abstract relationships among intercepted texts and public documents, and it can find even less distinct patterns.

Indeed, when NSA veteran William Black Jr. briefly retired from the intelligence agency in 1997, he went to SAIC for three years, but then returned to the NSA as deputy director in 2000. Two years later, SAIC won the $282 million job of overseeing the latest phase of Trailblazer, the most thorough revamping of the NSA's eavesdropping systems in its history.[255]

In a further Orwellian twist to the story of SAIC, the company ran a multi-billion-dollar sideline to their spy business. SAIC owed a media outfit that would be contracted to bring Iraqis their very own free press in the post-Saddam era.

PROPAGANDA FOR THE PEOPLE

Zainab Abdul Hameed, a reporter for the Iraqi Media Network's (IMN) Al Iraqiya radio and television station, trudged back from her daily visit to the oil ministry in Baghdad. She was waiting for news on two fronts but had nothing to report that day. Her assignment was to check on the electricity situation, but she was also waiting to hear if she still had a job. It was early December 2003 and she suspected, correctly as it turned out, that SAIC, her paymaster, would soon be fired if the rumors flying around the office were true.

"No news today, but maybe tomorrow," she told me cheerfully. Eight months after the ousting of Saddam Hussein, Iraq's basic infrastructure was still a shambles, despite billions of dollars apparently spent to fix it: Baghdad continued to suffer through ten hours of power cuts a day. "We are free to report whatever we want," said Hameed. "It's not like under Saddam Hussein when we had to report what the government told us to say."

To get to work Hameed had to walk through a maze of barbed wire, concrete barricades and three body searches run by the Florida National Guard and ISI, a private Iraqi security company. Her office was on the third floor of the Baghdad convention center where the United States military held press conferences about the occupation of her country. The fact that the Al Iraqiya's main office was right above the military was no coincidence—the military was their only funder. At the final checkpoint outside the entrance to the corridor that houses Al Iraqiya's offices, she passed a television that was almost always tuned to either Al Jazeera or Al Arabiya, the popular Middle Eastern satellite channels that were the IMN's main rivals.[256]

The Defense Contracting Command awarded the $15 million contract to run the Iraqi Media Network to SAIC on March 11, 2003, eight days before the invasion began, without any acquisition plan or competitive bidding. It justified the award by claiming that the company was the only acceptable contractor to take over Saddam Hussein's broadcast network and that there was an unusual and compelling urgency for the sole-source contract.[257]

As mentioned earlier in this chapter, SAIC is not a media company at all. The closest SAIC has gotten to running a television network is a contract to manage surveillance cameras at the Olympics.[258] But SAIC's Web site does offer a nine-point program of "Information Dominance/Command and Control," starting with "Battlefield Control" and ending with "Information Warfare/Information Operations." It was this military-media management skill that probably won SAIC the contract.[259]

PSYCHOLOGICAL WARFARE OR YESTERDAY'S INFORMATION?

Indeed, the first IMN programming was broadcast with a fuzzy TV signal streamed from United States Air Force EC-130E "Commando Solo" psychological operations (psy-ops) planes. IMN went on the air with radio broadcasts to southern Iraq from Kuwait. Regular radio programming began April 10, and television May 13, 2003.[260]

At the time, the IMN programming seemed to be a spectacular triumph in psychological warfare, but, like the rest of the invasion, the first giddy days soon proved a mirage. Within months SAIC's work came under criticism for its amateurish and propagandistic quality. In the streets of Basra and Baghdad, I asked people if they watch Al Iraqiya and the answer was almost invariably no. What was most surprising is that I got the same answer from people who hate Saddam Hussein and those who supported the Americans. Almost everybody got their news from Al Jazeera or Al Arabiya. "Al Iraqiya has no news. Just yesterday's information," was the common refrain.

Chagrined reporters at Al Iraqiya agreed, but said that strict rules issued by the occupation authorities banned them from reporting material that might incite violence. Don North, a correspondent who had worked in Vietnam, Washington, and the Middle East reporting for ABC and NBC News, called Al Iraqiya "Project Frustration" when he quit in July. "IMN has become an irrelevant mouthpiece for CPA propaganda, managed news, and mediocre programs. I have trained journalists after the fall of tyrannies in Bosnia, Romania, and Afghanistan. I don't blame the Iraqi journalists for the failure of IMN. Through a combination of incompetence and indifference, the CPA has destroyed the fragile credibility of IMN," he wrote in *Television Week*.[261]

North says that simple matters like a $500 request for a satellite dish to downlink the Reuters news feed was refused and a $200 request for printing a training manual that he put together in Arabic for reporters was turned down.

North was not the only senior staffer to quit. The first news director, Ahmad al Rikaby, proudly told the *Baghdad Bulletin*, "I opened my eyes to a family who were fighting Saddam Hussein and became part of this fight—I always wanted to speak freely in Iraq but never had a chance to do so. The project of creating free media in Iraq is an honor, a dream." But he too resigned when the occupation authorities rehired staff troublemakers as well as Ba'athists that he had fired.[262]

Meanwhile those reporters who stayed on were ordered to cover daily occupation authority news conferences, interviews, and photo opportunities while being paid the equivalent of $120 a month, the paucity of which led to major strikes by the reporters.[263]

That December I met with Alaa Fa'ik, an Iraqi American from Ann Arbor, Michigan, who was the second in command at the IMN. Dressed casually in a sweater, with short-cropped, gray hair and glasses, with a military-issued badge identifying him as a SAIC employee hanging on a blue strap around his neck, he insisted that it was a popular network.

"I am not in competition with Al Jazeera, let them do whatever they want to do. In fact, most Iraqis don't have satellite dishes. Those that do found the remote control to be a new toy. Now they are returning to us because they trust us to tell the truth. Freedom has to be exercised with respon-

164   PRATAP CHATTERJEE

sibility and we will not allow Saddam Hussein to use this as
a platform," he says. (At the time, despite the fact that not
everybody could afford a satellite dish, government surveys
showed that one in four Iraqis watched Al Jazeera and Al
Arabiya compared to less than one in ten for Al Iraqiya.)

Fa'ik also denies that the military had stifled their reporting.

> Yes, we are getting money from the Department of
> Defense. That is from you and me, the taxpayer.
> Are you reporting the fact that the Ministry of
> Education is funded by the United States govern-
> ment, the Ministry of Health is funded by the
> United States? I don't understand why when it
> comes to the media, you say, no, no, no. So who is
> going to fund it?
>
> The United States government took the respon-
> sibility of helping Iraq put foundations for democra-
> cy and change. So for them to support an independ-
> ent Iraqi television should be welcomed. Every
> penny spent on this project has been worthwhile,
> despite the fact that I work here, really we are going
> to [broadcast] independent television, not con-
> trolled by the state. In Iraq, in the Middle East, this
> is a new concept for a station to be sponsored by the
> government but independent of the state.[264]

ARMORED HUMVEES, CHARTERED JETS

Three months after I met Fa'ik, a report from the Pentagon's
Inspector General's office, painted a very different financial

picture. By the end of September, SAIC's costs under the contract had escalated from $15 million to $82.3 million. For example, the report said SAIC's media program manager tried to buy a Hummer H2 and a Ford C-350 pickup for his use on the contract and chartered a DC-10 cargo jet to fly the vehicles to Iraq. When a defense acquisition specialist refused to allow these items to be added to the contract, the manager "went around the authority of this acquisition specialist" to a high-level Pentagon office and got approval. SAIC was unable to pinpoint the exact cost of the airlifted vehicles, although one invoice titled "Office and Vehicle" totaled roughly $381,000. The inspector general's report also noted that one SAIC contractor was paid even though he was on vacation. In another, a "subject matter expert" hired for SAIC's media contract was put in charge of determining how to dispose of garbage in Iraq, before being assigned a role advising Iraq's Ministry of Youth and Sport.

The inspector general's report suggested that "In each phase . . . DCC-W (Defense Contracting Command-Washington) cut corners, from generating the initial requirements to surveillance of the contractor," recommending that "appropriate administrative action" be taken against officers who did not follow the rules.[265]

On January 9, 2004, the Pentagon awarded a $96 million contract to Harris Corporation of Melbourne, Florida, to take over the IMN project.[266] Technically, SAIC's contract was never canceled—it simply did not apply for the new contract. In February, the Broadcasting Board of Governors (BBG), which oversees all United States nonmilitary propaganda efforts such as the Voice of America, Radio Free Europe/Radio Liberty (RFE/RL), Radio Free Asia (RFA), and Radio and TV Marti, launched the Al-Hurra ("the Free One" in Arabic) satellite channel with more than $62 million in government funding, in an effort to create a channel resembling CNN, MSNBC, and the Discovery Channel.[267]

Judgement from the rest of the Arab media was quick. *Al Ahram*, one of the best known Arabic language papers, said, "It is difficult to understand how the U.S., with its advanced research centers and clever minds, explains away Arab hatred as a product of a demagogic media and not due to its biased policies and propensity to abuse Arab interests."

Once up and running the Al-Hurra channel quickly demonstrated its close ties to the administration. The first guest interviewed was none other than President George Bush—causing *Al Quds Al Arabi* newspaper to comment that rather than appearing free, the network "brought to mind official channels broadcast by regimes mired in dictatorship, just like those of the 1960s and beginning of the '70s."[268]

In December Fa'ik told me, "For me as an Iraqi American, I am on the two sides of the coin. As an Iraqi, I want the American money. As an American I want to [help] build an independent media. This is a concept that is new to the whole Middle East. This is an experiment. If it succeeds, it is going to set new rules for the media in the Arab world." Unfortunately both the Al Iraqiya and the Al Hurra experiment seem to have completely failed.

In April 2004, I met with Isam al-Khafaji, a dapper academic from the University of Amsterdam, who had grown up in the Adhamiya district of Baghdad. An occasional advisor to the Pentagon, the World Bank, and now the director of Iraq Revenue Watch (a tiny offshoot of the Open Society

Institute, the umbrella for George Soros's nonprofit empire), he had joined the IRDC but left after a few months.[269]

Al-Khafaji lit his cigarette and leaned back in his chair, as the waiter brought in plates of mixed grill kebabs. His little office, which resembled a doctor's spartan and sterile office, overlooking the Tigris in one of the oldest hotels in Baghdad, reminded me of colonial enclaves in Colombo or Calcutta: quiet and serene amid the chaos of the bustling city.

Bit by bit, the story unfolded. In 1997 al-Khafaji and others testified before Congress to get $5 million as part of the Iraq Liberation Act. The money was spent in the fall of 2002 to hold eighteen workshops organized jointly by the State Department and the Pentagon. Yet the two organizations approached their shared project with differing agendas.

One of the thirty-two key people at the "Future of Iraq" gathering was Munther al-Fadhal, a Shiite Muslim from the holy city of Najaf, who had worked as a law professor in Baghdad until he was forced to flee to Sweden after the 1991 Persian Gulf War for criticizing Iraq's occupation of Kuwait. Al-Fadhal presented a draft of an Iraqi constitution at the meeting.[270]

A major force behind these meetings was a group from Michigan called the Iraqi Forum for Democracy (IFD). As luck would have it, the rotating chairmanship of the IFD fell to a man named Emad Dhia, a fifty-one-year-old engineer and pharmaceutical executive from Pfizer who had left Iraq at the age of thirty and was presently living in Plymouth, Michigan. Although he had little experience in government and policy, Dhia, through his position as chairman, was parachuted into a key role for Iraq's future, in what will rank as one of the occupation's leading mistakes in planning the new Iraq.[271]

Soon after the hearings, Joanne Dickow, an Iraqi American aide to Spencer Abraham, the energy secretary and former senator from Michigan, heard Paul Wolfowitz, the deputy secretary of defense, talk about his hope of enlisting Arab-Americans in his campaign to rally sentiment against the Iraqi rulers. Dickow got in touch with Dr. Maha Hussein, an Ann Arbor, Michigan–based oncologist and professor at the University of Michigan, who was also a leading member of the forum. Hussein arranged for Wolfowitz and Dhia to meet.

After a series of meetings in the Detroit area between Iraqi exiles and Pentagon officials, the plans for the IRDC were drawn up at a February gathering at the Pentagon and finalized after a rally in Detroit on February 23, 2003, at which Wolfowitz was the main speaker.

"It's an enormously valuable asset to have people who share our values, understand what we're about as a country, and are in most cases citizens of this country, but who also speak the language, share the culture and know their way around Iraq," Wolfowitz said later.[272]

Over the next two months, Dhia took a primary role in organizing the IRDC, working closely with Victor Rostow, his liaison at the Pentagon. Rostow told *The New York Times* that SAIC was a useful cover for Iraqi Americans. "Most of these people believe that if they are seen as agents of America, they will be killed," he said.[273] Al-Khafaji says that it went beyond that to a question of if he could trust the U.S. government. "That was the hardest choice for me— should I work for the Pentagon? I am an Iraqi, and even though I was opposed to the war, I wanted to help rebuild my country. Many of the others felt the same way," he recalled.[274]

Dhia and Hussein were invited to the White House for a meeting with President George Bush on April 4, 2003, as part the president's larger consultation with Iraqi Americans. A government press release issued that day described Dhia thus:

In 1970, Emad [Dhia]'s aunt was accused of being a member of a group plotting to topple the Ba'ath government. Though she was the first woman to graduate from the University of Baghdad School of Medicine and a prominent doctor in Iraq, she was apprehended and put in jail. The next day Emad's father was arrested, but was released after three weeks. After spending two years in prison, his aunt was finally released. Less than a year later, she was assassinated while working in her clinic in Iraq.

Regarding Hussein, the press release stated

While attending the Baghdad University School of Medicine in the late 1970s, Maha [Hussein] witnessed the disappearance of many fellow medical students. After graduating in 1980, she and her husband left Iraq as fears of border closures mounted in advance of a possible war with Iran. Shortly after leaving Iraq, many of her family's neighbors in Baghdad were expelled from their homes and forced to flee to Iran. Two of her cousins that stayed behind were executed in the late 1980s for arranging to hide a Kurdish friend that was evading the regime's security forces. The male cousin who arranged for the hiding was shot and killed. The sister whose house he was hiding in was beaten to death, mutilated, and then paraded naked through a public area.[275]

Not everybody at the White House gathering was aware of the IRDC. Raz Rasool, from an advocacy group called Women for a Free Iraq, fled Iraq in 1998, seeking refuge in Fairfax, Virginia. She confessed her surprise almost a month after the meeting: "Many of us are really upset that we didn't know about this. They started this two months ago and we read about it just this week," she admitted.[276]

BUILDING A NEW BRAIN

Later, a total of 150 people were hired by the IRDC. Over the course of many meetings, they decided that four people would be assigned to each of Iraq's provinces or governorates as well as to each of Iraq's key ministries, where they were to work closely with American and British officials under Jay Garner, the retired lieutenant general who was initially appointed Iraq's day-to-day ruler. Each member of the team was dispatched by the Pentagon to American military bases, such as Fort Hood, Texas, to undergo several days of self-defense training.

Within a week of the White House gathering, Iraq descended into a frenzy of looting and chaos, signaling that the United States would have to take up the reins of the government immediately, despite the fact that plans at the IRDC and the Pentagon were, understandably, still sketchy. In hindsight, this lack of sufficient planning prior to a decision to launch a full-scale war, could be viewed as irresponsible— a surefire recipe for disaster—as indeed it later proved to be.

Exactly three weeks later, on Friday April 25, 2003, Dhia and nine others left for Kuwait and then Baghdad. The following week they would be joined by fifteen Iraqi expatriates for a meeting with designated Pentagon officials (many of whom were civilians pulled from academia and nonprofits and hired on the strengths of their resumes rather than their country of origin) to take charge of the key ministries of oil, planning, and industry.[277]

By this time it had become apparent that there was more than one agenda at play. The Pentagon systematically excluded State Department employees who had worked on the Future of Iraq Project, favoring it own staff with Iraq postings. For example, the original director, Tom Warrick, was invited by Garner to join his staff in Baghdad. Warrick had begun packing his bags, but Pentagon civilians vetoed his appointment.[278]

Fadhal was one of the chosen ones. He was dispatched to the Ministry of Justice in Iraq "to create the new legal system toward democracy that will accept human rights, that will fight corruption in Iraq, and create new laws to build democracy." Shortly before he left the Virginia base, he revealed his hopes to a *New York Times* reporter. "Maybe in five or six years they'll understand that this guy is a good guy," he said. Yet at the same time he was worried that Iraqis would see him "as an agent or a spy," so he arranged for six Kurdish bodyguards to meet him in Baghdad, to supplement his American military guards.

"I have a dream to build in Iraq a civil society, a democracy, like Switzerland or Sweden. But now there is chaos and risk—from Islamic fanatic groups, and from the Ba'ath Party and from the Arab terrorists who supported the Hussein government. The Iraqi people have been brainwashed and it is our responsibility to build a new brain," he said.

But from day one Iraqis, both in Iraq and abroad, viewed the experiment with deep suspicion. "This is insulting," Imam Husham al-Husainy, an Iraqi Shiite leader who runs the Karbala Islamic Education Center in Detroit told *The New York Times*. "Where is the democracy if you're just dictating our ideas? That's not democracy. Don't impose it on us."[279]

Al Khafaji says that once the group arrived in Baghdad, the collaboration soon melted away. As each individual became more and more involved in their appointed task and as security concerns mounted making it hard to move around Baghdad, the meetings of the larger group ceased. Some individuals left after a few short months, disappointed; others stayed on.

I DID NOT WANT TO BE A COLLABORATOR

On July 9, 2003, less than five months after the IRDC began operations, al Khafaji quit publicly. He subsequently spoke out, and then opted to stay in Baghdad and challenge the system. In an opinion article titled "I Did Not Want to Be a Collaborator," published in the *Guardian UK*, he wrote about the failing of the IRDC.

> I feared my role with the reconstruction council was sliding from what I had originally envisioned— working with allies in a democratic fashion—to collaborating with occupying forces.
>
> I had returned to Baghdad in May, a few weeks after the fall of Saddam Hussein, with much hope after 25 years in exile from my country. It was one of the most difficult decisions of my life to accept

the invitation of the U.S. government to return with more than 140 other Iraqis as part of this council to help with the postwar reconstruction and rehabilitation of ministries so that Iraq could eventually be turned over to a transitional government.

My understanding of this council, which first reported to retired general Jay Garner, and is now under civil administrator Paul Bremer, was that we would work with Iraq's ministries, not as ministers, but in the background as advisers. Its goal was to restore Iraq's badly damaged infrastructure—the electricity, the hospitals, the water supplies and the transportation routes—at least to its pre-war state so that the country could be turned over to a transitional government.

Though we council members came from all over the world, we are all Iraqis. I accepted the fact that we were a defeated country, and had no problem working with the U.S. But there seemed to be no interest on the part of the coalition in involving Iraqis as advisers on the future of their nation. Our role was very limited. Even reporters who visited us took note, writing that although the reconstruction council has an office within the presidential palace, there seems to be little done there apart from members reading their email.

There was euphoria when Baghdad first fell, but the Americans acted with arrogance. While many Iraqis are relieved to see Saddam out, and accept the fact that the U.S. is the only power than can secure some semblance of order, they now see it acting as an occupier.

Sadly, the vision for a transitional government
and democratic elections put forward by Wolfowitz
seems to have been forgotten in the everyday pressures of postwar Iraq. Wolfowitz is just one player
and there are many others on the ground in Iraq
who do not share his vision. Even the soldiers here
bluntly say they take their orders from their general, not from Bremer.

Bitter disputes between the defense department
and the state department continue to affect the situation. Even though Bremer has the formal authority within Iraq, it seems like each and every decision must go back to Washington, and we are the
victims of indecision.

Iraq is now in almost total chaos. No one knows
what is going on. We're not talking here about trying to achieve an ideal political system. People cannot understand why a superpower that can amass
all that military might can't get the electricity back
on. Iraqis are now contrasting Saddam's ability to
bring back power after the war in 1991 to the apparent inability of the U.S. to do so now. There are all
kinds of conspiracy theories.

Now Bremer has established the Iraqi Governing
Council. Sitting together to consider the future of
Iraq are 25 representatives, hand-picked by the US-
led coalition. The composition is not a bad one, but
few of the members have substantial domestic constituencies. Whether the council is effective or not
depends on whether its members are able to reach
any consensus. I fear they will be played against one
another.

> To succeed, they must take a unified position on issues and tell Bremer to go to Washington and say "this is what Iraqis want." Ultimately, the council must be prepared to say: "Give us full authority and we will ask for your advice when we need it."
>
> I am thus far the first and only member of the reconstruction council to resign. There may be others, though many will no doubt stay and hope for the best. For my part, when I think about the Iraqi people how strong they are, how hard they work I remain optimistic for my country in the medium term.
>
> There are many signs that Iraqis are working together, without serious tensions between ethnicities. All this is good news for a future Iraq. In the short term, however, I fear there will be more conflicts, run through with Iraqi and American blood.[280]

In mid-April 2004, nine months after he made this prediction, as the country slid into chaos with the military offensives in Falluja and Najaf, al Khafaji quietly left Iraq, making his way back to Amsterdam.

THE GREAT IRAQI PRIVATIZATION CAPER

While the administration was maneuvering behind the scenes to control the ministries and governorates with the help of their Iraqi-American advisors, they were much more blatant about their intention to sell off the Iraqi economy.

May Day is traditionally celebrated in most countries (with the notable exception of the United States) as Labor

Day, commemorating the 1886 protests in Chicago that eventually led to an eight-hour work day. On that day in 2003, notes from a confidential memo drafted by the Bush administration appeared in the *Wall Street Journal*, calling for major layoffs in the Iraqi public sector.[281]

The one-hundred-page document titled "Moving the Iraqi Economy from Recovery to Sustainable Growth," called for shutting down and selling the assets of heavily indebted Iraqi companies as well as offering tradable ownership vouchers to ordinary Iraqi citizens for more profitable state companies through "a broad-based Mass Privatization Program," similar to a program used in Russia in the mid-nineties.

The document suggests hiring a consultant to help support "private sector involvement in strategic sectors, including privatization, asset sales, concessions, leases, and management contracts, especially in the oil and supporting industries" that dominate Iraq's business activity.

USAID went ahead and hired what appeared to be an unknown company, called Bearing Point, based in McLean, Virginia. A quick search revealed that although the name was largely unknown to the general public, the company was not—Bearing Point is the name for the spin off of megaaccounting firm KPMG. (Following the collapse of accounting giant Arthur Andersen due to the conflict of interest in providing auditing as well as tax-dodging advice to Enron, most accounting firms distanced themselves from their consulting divisions by parting ways financially and giving the latter completely new names. In fact, Bearing Point hired many of the Arthur Andersen consultants who lost their jobs when the parent firm shut its doors.)

Bearing Point's three-year privatization process suggested the creation of a "world-class exchange," "a comprehensive income tax system consistent with current international practice," a new banking system that would incorporate the traditional Islamic money-transfer system, and "an extremely rapid and thorough exchange of currencies." To begin, the project sought to collect and destroy the old bills and replace them with new ones by July, 2004.

The memo met with widespread skepticism even from experts. "This will not be credible to the Iraqi people or anyone else if we try to do it ourselves. The World Bank and the IMF have a lot more experience and a lot more credibility in this than the U.S. government," said Edwin Truman, a former senior international finance official at the Federal Reserve who served in the Clinton administration's Treasury Department. He pointed to how rapid the privatization of state-run enterprises in the former Soviet Union led to sharp disruptions in jobs and services, as well as rampant corruption.

When the man hired to run Iraq said it wouldn't work, maybe the Bush administration should have thought twice about its plans. General Jay Garner later shared his concerns about the project with BBC *Newsnight*.

> What I was trying to do was get to a functioning government.... We as Americans like to put our template on things. And our template's good, but it's not necessarily good for everyone else. T.E. Lawrence has a great saying—I wish I could repeat it exactly, I can't, but it goes something like this: "It is better for them to do it imperfectly than for us to do it for them perfectly because in the end this is their country and you won't be here very long." I think that's good advice.

I think you would be hard pressed to go up north
and convince the Kurds they had to be privatized.
You can convince the Kurds that they ought to own
the oilfields, but the privatization, I don't think you
could convince them of that. That's just one fight
that you don't have to take on right now.

Rather, this opinion (together with his public call for
quick and free elections) led to Garner's hasty dismissal.
"The night I got to Baghdad, [Defense Secretary Donald]
Rumsfeld called me and told me he was appointing Paul
Bremer as the presidential envoy.... The announcement...
was somewhat abrupt."[282]

The USAID plan went ahead and was partially successful.
Bearing Point hired the New Jersey–based engineering firm
Louis Berger Group as a subcontractor to oversee the collection and destruction of old Iraqi currency and the introduction of a new one, which was completed before the end of
spring 2004.

But on privatization, Bearing Point did not fare well,
despite the full backing of Bremer and his staff—notably
Thomas Foley, the director of private sector development for
the occupation authorities, a Harvard buddy of George W.
Bush, and chairman of Bush's Connecticut campaign finance
committee in 2000.[283]

In late June 2003, Bremer outlined his vision for a free-market Iraq before hundreds of executives attending a meeting of
the World Economic Forum in Jordan. "Markets allocate
resources much more efficiently than politicians. So our
strategic goal in the months ahead is to set in motion policies
which will have the effect of reallocating people and resources
from state enterprises to more productive private firms."

On September 19, 2003, Bremer issued a rule known as Order 39 that allowed foreign investors to fully own Iraqi companies with no requirements for reinvesting profits back into the country, a move that had previously been restricted, under the Iraqi constitution, to citizens of Arab countries. The only industry that was exempted from privatization was the oil industry, which, as Garner pointed out, would never have been accepted by the Iraqi public.

Under Executive Order 13303, signed by President George W. Bush in late May 2004, Iraqi oil contractors were given a lifetime exemption from lawsuits. This order applied to Iraqi oil products that are "in the United States, hereafter come within the United States, or that are or hereafter come within the possession or control of United States persons."

"In other words, if ExxonMobil or ChevronTexaco touch Iraqi oil, anything they or anyone else does with it is immune from legal proceedings in the U.S.," explained Jim Vallette, an analyst with the Sustainable Energy & Economy Network of the Institute for Policy Studies in Washington, D.C.

"Anything that has happened before with oil companies around the world—a massive tanker accident; an explosion at an oil refinery; the employment of slave labor to build a pipeline; murder of locals by corporate security; the release of billions of tons of carbon dioxide into the atmosphere; or lawsuits by Iraq's current creditors or the next true Iraqi government demanding compensation—anything at all, is immune from judicial accountability," he said.[284]

The new laws sparked a little gold rush in Washington, D.C. Joe Allbaugh, President Bush's 2000 campaign manager, set up an advisory firm of Republican lobbyists to help American companies acquire distribution rights for everything from grain to auto parts to shampoo. "Getting the rights to distribute Procter & Gamble products would be a gold mine. One well-stocked 7-Eleven could knock out 30 Iraqi stores; a Wal-Mart could take over the country," one of the partners at New Bridge told the *Washington Post*. Another lobbying firm run by Bob Livingston, former Republican congressman from Louisiana and House Appropriations Committee chairman, represented well-placed Iraqi families looking for joint ventures with foreign companies to set up local operations.

Critics denounced the greed. "It's like a huge pot of honey that's attracting a lot of flies," said John McCain, a Republican senator from Arizona.[285] But there was no check-ing the enthusiasm of the privatizers. In October, Foley held a conference call with reporters at the Pentagon, in which he said he would present the Iraqi Governing Council with a proposal on privatizing state-owned businesses within seven months. Foley's plan was to sell off 150 of the 200 state-owned enterprises in Iraq (which employed a half-million Iraqi workers)—but exclude electricity assets and financial institutions, such as state-owned banks and insurance com-panies as well as the oil industry. Firms Foley wanted to sell off included cement companies, fertilizer operations, a phos-phate mining operation, sulfur mining and extraction busi-nesses, pharmaceutical companies, and the airline and auto-mobile tire makers.

"Although it is a large task in Iraq, in overall terms it's not nearly as big a task as it was in most of the eastern bloc countries, both in terms of the number of companies and the percent of the work force that's affected," said Foley.[286]

A couple of days later, he met with reporters in Baghdad to expand on this idea. "We selected a small group, fewer than ten SOEs [state-owned enterprises] that are very small and very simple, low-asset businesses to begin initial privatization steps," he said.[287]

But behind the scenes, things were not going well. One of the first SOEs to be put on the auction block met with almost immediate disaster. The State Company for Vegetable Oils, one of forty-eight companies in the Ministry of Industry, owned six factories that produced cheap consumer goods, ranging from partially hydrogenated cooking oil to shampoo and detergent. The government subsidized imports of raw materials, charging the company only one dollar for every six thousand dollars' worth of materials brought in.

American experts who examined the company over the summer decided on an easy first step—stop the government subsidies and offer private investors the opportunity to run the company, with complete freedom to make strategic business decisions from shutting down older factories and firing redundant employees to bring costs under control, as well as overseeing the purchase of raw materials and sale of finished products at market prices. The vegetable oil company's director at the time, Faez Ghani Aziz, was enthusiastic. "We need outside investors. We cannot continue like this," he said.

Aziz fired dozens of workers. Then, all of sudden, the plan went awry. Aziz was shot and killed on his way to work, sending a wave of panic through the Ministry of Industry, which immediately put all the other privatization plans on hold.[288] Other SOE managers announced their opposition to the plans. Dathar al-Kashab, manager of the Al Daura oil refinery, said: "I'll have to fire 1500 [of the refinery's 3000] workers. In America when a company lays people off, there's unemployment insurance, and they won't die from hunger. If I dismiss employees now, I'm killing them and their families."[289]

By December, with little support from inside Iraq, Foley called another press conference at the Pentagon. "The [privatization] process is a long one and my guess is that it will be several years before any significant privatizations are done and it is also my guess that most of these businesses will end up being owned by Iraqis," he said in a conference call to reporters.

"The implementation and the timing of the privatization will be in the future and will be the role of a sovereign government in Iraq," he added, without specifying which firms would likely be privatized first.[290]

By February 2004, Foley admitted he had lost. The Iraqi Governing Council had completely rejected his plan for privatization. He started to backpedal furiously on the promises he made in 2003. "There never would have been a plan to sell off state enterprises to foreigners. It would have been to Iraqis," Foley told Reuters. He said that Ministry of Industry had been unable to even lease out the management of SOEs.

He left Iraq at the end of the month, reassigned to promoting private sector investment in Iraq abroad.[291] He made stump speeches pointing to the explosive demand in Iraq for satellite dishes like in Europe and the United States. "Most every balcony has a satellite dish hanging from it. They've done a very effective job of penetrating the market. I think the replacement for the satellite dishes is the cell phone.... [There is a] block-long line of Iraqis waiting to buy them."[292] Finally, in March, Foley was quietly laid off and returned to Connecticut to his investment firm, the NTC group.[293]

INVENTING DEMOCRACY IN NORTH CAROLINA

So much for planning the ministries and attempting to hive off the profitable aspects of government. The thorny problem of elections was a much bigger dilemma facing the occupation authorities. Had elections been held the day after "liberation," there was no guarantee that the Iraqis might not vote back the Ba'athists for fear that the Americans might abandon them, as they had in the past. Another fear was that the Shia majority would overwhelm the Sunnis minority and provoke a civil war. Overhanging all of this was the fact that Iraq's neighbors, Saudi Arabia and Iran, are run by powerful religious groups with no great like for the United States. The United States feared Iraq might gradually be converted into a fundamentalist state.

No, reasoned the Washington mandarins, democracy needed to be introduced gradually and molded to follow the American system. This would allow the participation of all: women, tribal minorities, and maybe even religious groups. For this they turned to Research Triangle Institute International (RTI) of North Carolina, a think tank set up in 1958 to market research from local universities. USAID awarded a $167 million contract to RTI to bring democracy to 180 Iraqi cities and towns, the largest grant that the think tank had won in its forty-five-year history.

RTI started hiring right away. A Mormon preacher from Utah, a city manager from Houston, and a professor of anthropology from New York City were dispatched to Iraq for the grand experiment—or was it really a grand conspiracy to invent a sympathetic body of Iraqi public officials to appoint a regime that would be friendly to the United States?

"Early elections can often lead to violence," RTI chief Ronald Johnson said.[294] To avoid this, RTI used a plan that it had tried in a limited manner in Indonesia and El Salvador. Johnson explained the process to Naomi Klein, a Canadian journalist reporting from Iraq for the *Guardian* thus:

> There really is not a Sunni way to pick up the garbage vs. a Shiite way, vs. a Syrian way to pick up the garbage. Local government services are, in many ways, pretty cut-and-dried. There's a lot of politics about how much you do, and there's certainly politics about picking up the garbage in one neighborhood and not picking it up in another neighborhood.
>
> So our foundation, if you will—the way we approach Iraq as well (and then obviously our contract is local government)—is to say that what we're first trying to do is work on making sure services get delivered, and that they get delivered pretty efficiently and effectively, and that people can observe that—you know, what the local government is or is not doing.
>
> The way we helped form a neighborhood council is to hold a meeting of as many people in the neighborhood as we could get to come to the meeting. Announcements are distributed, people are invited, they're urged to bring people and you have kind of a town meeting. Only it's a town meeting that in a lot of cases covers a small geographic area, but its potential is for a lot of the adult residents of that neighborhood to actually physically come together in a meeting, in person.[295]

FROM UTAH, A MAN OF GOD

RTI hired James Mayfield, a seventy-year-old professor emeritus at the University of Utah who had just completed a three-year stint running a Church of Latter Day Saints mission in the Houston suburbs. He ran his classes at Hilla, eighty miles south of Baghdad, in a crypt-like room at the rear of a huge mosque that Hussein built to his own glory at the closing passage of his twenty-four–year rule. Mayfield was in charge of Babil, Karbala, Najaf, Qadisiyah, and Wasit districts.

Many Iraqis were invited to these classes and the council meetings that RTI organized, and initially many came, although one might question their motives for attending. Indeed Mayfield described an incident in Hilla in his email blog on August 3, 2003, in which he encountered an audience willing to ask tough questions.

> Last night I went to one of these neighborhood council meetings. About 100 people came to a local school where I made a presentation. I talked about the possibility of establishing a democratic system in their neighborhood. Many of them stood up and spoke; even one woman had the courage to stand. Finally a young man, 17 or 18 stood up and asked me a tough question. How will democracy help me find a job?
>
> I told him that when the dictatorship in Japan was destroyed after World War II, the Japanese people had to wait nearly 9 years before they had a functioning democracy. And now they are one of

the richest countries in the world. I said to the young Iraqi, "If you ask a Japanese man, 'was it worth waiting nine years to have a democracy in Japan,' all Japanese will say yes it was worth the wait." Then I said, "Please be patient, it will not take nine years, probably or 2 or 3 years. Can you be patient?" He said, "No, I need money now!!"

I then stopped the conversation and said to all the people in the meeting, "Please note this young man, he is the future of Iraq. He stood up with courage, faced me and asked me a tough question. This is what democracy is about. If this boy had stood up and asked a hard question under Saddam Hussein, he probably would have been shot." Then I said, "I want to congratulate this young man, I want to applaud his courage."

Suddenly the whole audience stood up and openly applauded this young man. He was smiling so happily and I gave him a thumbs up sign and he returned it to me and I knew I had made a friend.[296]

When Mayfield went to the neighborhood council meeting the next time, he found out that this young man had been elected to be the council member for his neighborhood. He observed: "Someday he will be a leader in Iraq."

Critics might see the incident more cynically, guessing that many who attended these trainings and meetings were there to seek jobs or power, not to participate in democracy. Another example of the motives of the attendees comes from John Burns of *The New York Times* who was invited to attend one of Mayfield's classes in December, where he met Sayed Farqad al-Qiswini, the president of the theological col-

lege who took over the Hilla mosque after the invasion.
Qiswini told him, "We are chameleons," boasting that one
year prior he could have been found at the mosque singing
the praises of Saddam Hussein. (Indeed today Qiswini is a
local strongman for Moqtada al Sadr, the radical young cleric that has since become the bane of the American occupation.)[297]

But Mayfield, a committed Mormon, who prayed regularly with local soldiers, was convinced that he was wanted in
Iraq and that the experiment was succeeding. In his email
blog, he quoted Steven Vincent from the *National Review*:

> "We might follow the example of some Baghdadi
> diners I recently overheard who, when asked how
> they viewed the 'occupation,' replied, 'Occupation?
> This is a liberation.'" The predictions of doom and
> gloom have all but fizzled, yet the media continue
> to focus on incidents that make it appear the U.S.
> effort is failing. The reality is the bombings in Iraq
> hurt the civilians there far worse than they do the
> U.S. forces. The attacks are not against the United
> States occupation, they are against the people of
> Iraq who are making a brave and bold move towards
> democracy. Oil production is up, wages are increas-
> ing, consumer goods are filling the shelves, public
> services are better and, according to a Washington
> Times report, nearly a million more Iraqis have cars
> since Hussein was overthrown.

RTI soon rewarded Mayfield with a very fancy car of his
own on January 12, 2004, which he described as

A $200,000 all bullet proof car because I am the regional director and I have to travel all over the region on a regular basis. The windows are two inches thick; it is completely enclosed with three radios, a siren, built in loud speaker to call for help, and all leather seats. These are built for ambassadors and have special tires that can drive even if hit with a bullet. Now I have been here almost 8 months and never once has anyone shot at me but I have had to wear a thick, very heavy, very uncomfortable bullet proof vest. In the 8 months, I never had to use it. Thank goodness. Now I won't have to wear my vest anymore. They can shoot at me all day and I will be perfectly safe.[298]

Despite Mayfield's convinction regarding his work, RTI trainees in Iraq were skeptical of his methods. Jerry Kuhaida, a former mayor from Tennessee, told me: "I got this feeling that it was his last hurrah and he wasn't really open to any other ideas. It was his way or no way, but the problem was that his way was an academic way. I've spent fifteen years in city government, and I'm not sure his was would even work in the United States."

Kuhaida also related horror stories of how Mayfield would use critical military resources to distribute the medical supplies that the Mormons donated to his community. "We never asked for them, and in fact we never got what we had asked for," he said. "Instead, we had to spend a phenomenal amount of money—tens of thousands of dollars—transporting this stuff under armed guard. And a lot of it just ended up stacked up in my driveway and I had to figure out who to give it to."[299]

FROM TEXAS, A MAN WITH A BIG PENSION

Mayfield's counterpart in Baghdad was a man by the name of Al Haines who had also just arrived from Houston. Unlike the retired preacher, he was a former city official who had quit his job after having quietly used his position to triple his own pension and endured a string of embarrassing failures to balance the city budget.

Haines, the City of Houston's chief administrative officer, resigned from his job and went to Iraq to lead a team advising the city of Baghdad just over two months before his former boss, Mayor Lee Brown, having completed the maximum of three terms in office, was to step down.[300] He left behind ongoing complaints about his inability to solve the city's fiscal crisis, which dogged the mayor and himself.

For example at the end of 2000, Haines had to beg for a last minute loan—$8 million borrowed from the City's health benefits fund and $1 million from workers' compensation—so the City could pay almost nine thousand police officers and firefighters on December 29. "It's beyond me how something like that could happen. It's not like making payroll is a surprise," Councilwoman Annise Parker said. Haines's defense was that there were strict rules on how much cash the city can have on hand without facing a penalty from the Internal Revenue Service. But that past June, the city council was forced to vote on a transfer of $30 million between funds, in part to pay employees, two days before paychecks went out. And in 1999, the city faced a cash shortfall of $38 million after overestimating tax revenues.[301]

Bad fiscal management has plagued most cities in the

United States, but what makes Haines somewhat unusual was that under his watch the pension board strapped the city government with a $1.3 billion debt in 2003 that was projected to hit $1.8 billion by 2009.

A *Houston Chronicle* analysis published in March 2004, five months after Haines departed, showed that his pension rose from $36,000 a year under the old 1998 plan, negotiated before he took office, to $103,000 under the new 2003 plan, which he was in charge of negotiating. As calculated by the *Chronicle*, Haines is projected to receive 71.3 percent of his final salary of $145,000 for his 10.9 years with the city. Had the rules stayed as they were in 1998, he would be getting just under 25 percent. In an e-mail interview conducted with the *Chronicle*, Haines said most pension changes during the Brown administration were made to compensate for extremely low salaries earned by city workers.

While the city officials fumed, Haines was almost half a world away, living on Saddam Hussein's son's palatial property. ("Government is not here to make a few people rich," Shelly Sekula-Gibbs, a furious Houston city council member, told *Channel 11 News*.)[302] As far as Haines was concerned the two cities were pretty similar. "In Houston, we have 88 neighborhoods, and in Baghdad you have 88 neighborhoods," he said. And he marveled at the fact that people had similar discussions at meetings. "The similarities are unbelievable. People make their arguments, and I've heard them before," he told a *Cox News Service* reporter.[303]

When RTI officials dispatched Ibrahim Mustafa Hussain, the deputy mayor of Baghdad overseeing the city's water and sewer system, on a tour of Houston, he marveled at the same similarities. "It's about 88 councils [we] have.... The second thing, the city is flat, like Baghdad. And the services what you have in Houston are similar to what we have. I mean, the sewer network—same equipment. We use the same thing. We have the same problems with the roads they have," he told National Public Radio.[304]

But there are some crucial differences between the two cities. For one, city officials in Houston are elected by the residents, while in Baghdad they were appointed by the occupation authorities and managed by RTI. Another major difference is that neither the local councils nor the city council of Baghdad control budgets.

SELECTIONS NOT ELECTIONS

In May 2003, less than a month after the invasion was complete, elections for the disputed city of Mosul in the northern Iraq were held. The military allocated ten of the eighteen council seats to the city's Arab majority, with three seats for Kurds, two for Christians, and one each for Turkmen, Assyrian Christians, and Yezidis. But in a pattern that was repeated across Iraq, the members of the council were chosen by a group of about two hundred prominent local leaders, not a "one person, one vote" system, thus disenfranchising the majority of local people.[305]

RTI worked closely with the military occupation authorities to establish these new "democratic" city councils. For example, in December RTI officials in Rumaytha, in the province of Muthanna, finalized a city council with the help of the military. Initially posters were placed around town asking for the names of suitable candidates for a town council. The list was vetted by an eight-man council that the occupying American troops appointed in April 2003. From the list of submissions, the council selected one hundred

people to the town hall to vote on who would sit on the
council. The first vote produced a city manager who then
handled the rest of the proceedings. A town council was created consisting of seven members, each responsible for a different sector such as health, water and sewage, or security.[306]

The idea was to engage the local people in a semipopular
"appointocracy" at the local level that could be sold to the
world at large as a first step towards democracy. The system
appeared to be deliberately mixing the idea of public participation (anyone could submit names) with a degree of voting
(limited to those who had been vetted from the list of submitted names), which required approval by the military
before any final authority was awarded.

The occupation authorities hoped that would then allow
them to create a new five-tier council system that would not
reject the American overseers. These neighborhood councils
would select district councils, which, in turn would select
county councils, which, in turn would select a provincial
council, which, finally, would select a governor. Bingo! An
entirely new political system that would support the occupation and provide some measure of "grassroots" representation.

While these experiments in "democracy" were being tested, many Iraqis, believing that they were now free to organize their own affairs, started to have real elections. But in
late June, most of the U.S. military commanders, including
Major General Ray Odierno, commander of the Fourth
Infantry Division who was in charge of the northern half of
Iraq, ordered a halt to local elections and self-rule. Paul
Bremer told an interviewer, "Elections that are held too
early can be destructive. It's got to be done very carefully."

But the military clearly wasn't careful enough. Iraqi generals and police colonels, who had close ties to the Ba'ath Party, were appointed mayors of a dozen cities, including Samarra, Najaf, Tikrit, Balad and Baqubah. Mayor Abdul Munim Abud, a former artillery colonel, was appointed mayor of Najaf. Nabel Darwish Mohamed, a former colonel in the Iraqi police corps, was appointed mayor of nearby Balad while Samarra's mayorship was handed over to Shakir Mahmud Mohammad, a retired general from the Iraqi army.

Iraqis were furious. "They give us a general. What does that tell you, eh? First of all, an Iraqi general? They lost the last three wars! They're not even good generals. And they know nothing about running a city," Bahith Sattar, a biology teacher and tribal leader in Samarra who was a candidate for mayor until the election was canceled for the second time, told the *Washington Post.* "The new mayors do not have to be perfect. But I think that by allowing us to establish our own governments, many of the problems today would be solved. If you ask most Iraqis today if they have a government, they will tell you, no, what we have is an occupation, and that is a dangerous thing for the people to think," he added.[307]

GOING BACKWARDS

In Taji, a short distance north of Baghdad, the RTI advisors (led by Amal Rassam, an Iraqi American anthropology professor from New York) arrived with maps and flowcharts to oversee a "selection" process, only to discover that the local people had already chosen their own leaders.

The confusion at RTI was partly the fault of the military, says RTI's Johnson, who traveled to Taji in the early days of the occupation.

The local lieutenant colonel commanding the artillery battalion stationed at the military base there met with the tribal chiefs and wanted a group of people to help set priorities for some projects—school reconstruction, and so forth—and needed a group of people so it wouldn't be the U.S. saying, "these are the schools we're going to rebuild". He needed a group of Iraqis to say, "these are the schools." And he said, this is what we're going to do. We're going to rebuild the schools. We have some other projects that we're going to do, and we need you to tell us which are the most important to you. You have to help pick them out. And it was largely the tribal leaders of that area. As far as any-one could tell, it was a pretty representative group of those tribal chiefs. And he basically said, you guys, elect yourself a council. And they did.[308]

In the *Washington Post* Lieutenant Anthony Funkhouser, commander of the Fifth Engineer Battalion based at Fort Leonard Wood, Missouri, described the process between U.S. solidiers and Iraqis, saying, "We went to the village and said: 'Who is in charge? You need representation. Select four to five individuals." Further the paper reported

Within a week, the citizens had held an election. More than 600 men participated, and their votes were tallied on a blackboard at a nearby girls' school…. Several dozen people ran and five were elected. The villagers came back to Funkhouser with a memo listing the men and certifying that the people recognized them as their leaders.

Funkhouser went to the home of Rahman Hamarahim, the former mayor and newly elected head of the neighborhood council. Over Pepsi and kebabs one summer afternoon, the two men negotiated a sort of peace accord. The military would help the village repair its schools and clinics and find jobs. In exchange, Hamarahim and the other leaders would talk to insurgents about stopping their attacks and pass on information about hidden weapons caches. It has worked out well so far, both sides say. The public buildings now have gleaming new fans and new desks. The electricity is back on. The area is now one of the most peaceful in the district, and soldiers freely exchange high-fives and candy with the locals.[309]

When Rassam arrived on October 30, she was surprised to discover that there were already eleven neighborhood councils in the rural areas and a larger area group that called itself the Taji City Council, consisting mostly of prominent business leaders. "There is a lot of misinformation, competing interests, and high expectations which need to be reconciled," she said, telling the local people that they would have to start over using the RTI model. Saddam Abdul-Rahman Zaidan, a member of the Taji City Council, was very upset. "We will waste a whole month at least, and for what?" he asked. "We feel we are going backwards," another man protested.

Several local leaders, including Sabah Zaidaq, nicknamed the "sheik of sheiks" by U.S. soldiers and said to represent up to half the population of Taji, decided not to work with RTI or the military for fear of being seen as collaborators.

Others, such as Kamal Kiwan Abdul Ridha, the Taji council
president, said that RTI's reorganization was a plot by the
Ba'athists to return to power. "The plan was [created] by
some betrayers connected to the former regime," he
alleged.[310]

SADR CITY

In Sadr City, a teeming slum of some two million people on
the edge of Baghdad notorious for having nursed a great deal
of anger towards the Americans, the "appointocracy" system sparked protests and ended in bloodshed. First, the military and RTI helped select representatives to work in the
district council building, but soon after some ten thousand
supporters of Moqtada al Sadr kicked the appointed council
out and installed a rival council. "The Americans ran this
process; we didn't even know they were going to be selecting a council. So that's why the people of Sadr City rejected
them and elected us," Naim al-Kabi, an engineer and chairman of the rival council, told the *Christian Science Monitor.*

"We totally reject the council the American [soldiers]
helped create. If they'd sent civilians to talk to me, I'd be
more willing to listen," says Hussein D'eiyin al-Alawi, the
head of the Sadr City branch of the Daawa Party, a Shiite
political group.

On October 16, 2003, U.S. soldiers and local Iraqi police
brought in tanks, forced Kabi's council out of the building
and reinstalled their council. "The Sadr bureau people have
been making people suffer. We are the people's legitimate
representatives, and we've been bringing them aid and medicine. The Sadr people stopped that," said Siham Hittab, a
professor of English literature who taught James Joyce at

Baghdad University and one of the few women elected to the first council.[311]

On November 9, 2003, Kabi returned to the building and demanded to be allowed in. He refused to submit to what he saw as a humiliating weapons search and got into a "shoving match" with a U.S. soldier, who shot him dead, sparking more protest marches.

The American soldiers tried to pass off the electoral disaster in Sadr as naiveté on their part. "The good Lord knows we've screwed this thing up from the get-go, but He also knows every one of us has our heart in the right place, and I think the Iraqis feel that, too. We all want to help the Iraqis build something better than what they're coming out of, that's why it can be so upsetting when there's a setback. Sometimes it can seem so slow going," Major Paul Gass, a University of Houston ROTC teacher, told the *Monitor*.[312]

TOP DOWN TO TOP DOWN

"The point of these councils is to move the country from a top-down system where everything was ordered and based on oppression to one where ordinary Iraqis take on the task of representing citizens, not controlling them. It's a test for democracy. Can it work here?" asks Imad Jonaby, an Iraqi American working for RTI in Sadr City.[313]

What the RTI officials and the occupation authorities seemed to completely disregard was the fact that the use of the military to impose a council, in the face of local opposition, was not that different from the system imposed by Saddam Hussein, except that the dictator was more effective in suppressing dissent.

Several council officials have abandoned their posts, fearing future problems. In February 2004, Siham had advanced through the RTI system from Sadr City Council to a seat on the larger district council, and then to the more important Baghdad City Council. In February she decided to contest a seat on the Baghdad Provincial Council, the highest tier of the newly installed local government system, but then lost her nerve at the last moment. "These are two evils and we have to choose one of them. It is very difficult that the Iraqis have had to suffer all these years and now they have to suffer more. People really feel upset because they don't see any change in their lives."[314]

It is true that the new system has brought many ordinary Iraqis to power. For example, Ali Haidary, a mechanical engineer who owns an air conditioning repair company in the middle-class area of Al Adl, went to his local council to vote, not to run. But someone nominated him for a spot on his neighborhood council and he won, and he felt it was his responsibility to serve his people. In the weeks following his election, Haidary was elected to represent Al Adl on the Mansoor District Council, which in turn voted him onto the Baghdad City Council. In July 2003, he was elected vice chairman of the city council. Then in January 2004, he was appointed chairman of the political system that comprises eighty-eight individual councils and more than 750 representatives.[315]

He now has to fear for his life because of his role in the American-led political process; many of his colleagues at the local and city level have been targets of protests, attacks, and suicide bombings.

On April 19, 2004, the occupation authorities decided to take the next step in the political process in Baghdad. Forty-nine local government representatives were invited to a heavily guarded municipal building to choose a mayor. Not surprisingly they picked an Iraqi expatriate, Alaa Mahmood al Tamimi, an Iraqi engineer and academic who had returned from exile in the United Arab Emirates.[316] The final approval of his selection, however, was awarded to Paul Bremer.

WILL THINGS FALL APART?

At the end of the first twelve months, RTI had racked up $156 million in invoices to the U.S. government. In March 2004, the company was given a new one-year contract worth up to $154 million. Asked why the company had been awarded a new contract three months before other USAID contractors, Johnson told a local North Carolina newspaper, "If there are disruptions in services, that could disrupt the handover of sovereignty, and the new Iraqi government could have more trouble."[317]

But, given how manipulative the RTI system of "democracy" has been so far, the question is whether this system itself is likely to be one of the causes of protests and disruption. Anecdotal evidence suggests that most Iraqis have not participated in the RTI process. A National Public Radio reporter noted that, in February 2004, in Baqubah, an hour's drive north of Baghdad, only 2 percent of the city's ten thousand residents decided to participate in an election designed by Omar Abud, a Syrian Canadian who worked for RTI.[318] Herbert Docena, from the Bangkok-based nongovernmental organization, Focus on the Global South, told me that while the system was not rigged by RTI, it was deeply flawed.

> For the councils I observed, I think they really didn't have the luxury of choosing. They just cast the

net wide and made do with anyone willing to cooperate with them. I guess that's a self-selecting
process in itself, which weeds out the Sadr people
or the militants. Everyone admitted—and no one
denied—that the military and the RTI had the final
say on the selection. I guess they're still in the
process of gathering data on people at this stage; I
suspect they'd be handpicking people later, for the
more crucial positions.[319]

In search of these "legitimate" leaders, RTI employees
have been going around the country presiding over local
council meetings and organizing "democracy training
workshops" in which they exhort their fellow Iraqis to tell
their neighbors to trust the occupation forces and to support their plans for them. In one such workshop, a partici-
pant asked, "What's the use of the elections? Everyone
knows that the U.S. will be appointing our leaders anyway."
The RTI staff replied, "You must talk with people in your
neighborhood and tell them this is not true. The new elections will be honest, democratic, and free." She then
addressed the participants, saying, "You must tell your
neighbors to be patient. We were patient for thirty-five
years. What is another one-and-a-half years even if the situation now is very bad?"[320]

Bremer himself revealed his discomfort at elections, saying, "I'm not opposed to it but I want to do it in a way that
takes care of our concerns.... Elections that are held too early
can be too destructive....In a situation like this, if you start
holding elections, the people who are rejectionists tend to
win."[321] A senior official from the occupation authority was
more to the point when asked why elections couldn't be

held soon enough. "There's not enough time for the moderates to organize," he said.[322]

LOTS OF SPENDING, LITTLE WORK

The consultancy, however, judging by company press releas-
es, has a more optimistic view of what it achieved
"Throughout the first year, our in-country team of roughly
2,000 Iraqis and 200 international development specialists
worked in 18 governorates on a wide range of locally selected priorities ranging from increasing access to basic utilities
and healthcare to establishing and training local governing
councils," states an RTI press release.[323]

But three former RTI employees I spoke with who
worked on the project were less unequivocal about the company's success. They criticized the company for giving out
plenty of advice and holding many meetings, instead of
working to provide support for local community organizations or councils.

Jabir Algarawi, a Shiite from Diwaniya, had fled Iraq in
1991 to Arizona after taking part in an uprising to overthrow
Saddam Hussein that was called for by the first President Bush.
In December 2003, Algarawi, who supported the invasion of
Iraq, quit his job as executive director of the Arizona Refugee
Community Center in Phoenix and took a position with RTI.
Quicklyhe was flown to Al Amarah, the capital of Maysan
province in southeastern Iraq, to help Iraqis establish local
governance. At first, he said, "almost 95 percent of the people
[in the south] supported us. Now there are only a few, and
those who do don't have the courage to say it." He believes
that the lack of tangible support for local communities is one
of the principal reasons for the withdrawal of popular support.

Algarawi said that the only project he was able to finish was the creation of a women's organization, for which RTI allocated ninety thousand dollars in spending money. "We spent more than that on entertainment for our staff alone, bringing in satellite television," he said. "Many of the expatriate staff individually earned twice or three times as much money as the annual budget of this organization. Probably we spent 90 percent of our money on RTI staff and very little on the community."[324]

Algarawi also said that the RTI expatriate staff spent most of their time at their protected compound. "Some of my colleagues never left the compound; they spent all their time filling out forms for the United States government. It seemed like our main objective was satisfy our funders not to help people in Iraq," he said. "Those of us who did go outside, were told we could not go anywhere without our four Australian bodyguards, but that made the local people afraid of us. Many people said we were CIA and especially since we were not supposed to speak to the media, this did nothing to dispel the rumors."

He added that the company, whose supervisors stayed at the posh Sheraton hotel in Kuwait, bought supplies, from food to televisions, from Kuwait, not Iraq. "[We] gave no money to Iraqi organizations, [so] local people started to say that they needed to get Saddam to get the Iraqi money back from Kuwait," Algarawi said.

In early April 2004, Algarawi and all the other expatriate staff were told to evacuate Iraq because of the escalating violence. Then in late May, he heard that what little he had achieved might soon be undone. Dr. Kifaya Hussein, a staff member of the women's organization that he had helped establish, was gunned down in front of the office. "When she was killed, RTI didn't pay out the money they had promised, so now all the women are just volunteers," he said.

The paucity of resources for actual community initiatives was confirmed by Jerry Kuhaida, the former mayor of Oak Ridge, Tennessee, who had also resigned from his job in the United States to work for RTI in late 2003. He was assigned to Karbala, a city of five hundred thousand people about sixty miles south of Baghdad.

Kuhaida was put in charge of determining how money had been spent in the south central region, spanning four of Iraq's eighteen governorates. He calculated that RTI had given away eight to ten grants of between five thousand and fifty thousand dollars each. "It was all fluff," Kuhaida said. "We weren't really doing anything for the local organizations."[325]

But Patrick Gibbons, a spokesperson for RTI in Baghdad, disagreed with Algarawi and Kuhaida, arguing that the local grant-making program was successful. "The original LGP (local governance program) budget had $10 million allocated for grants to support local projects. The grant program was so successful that LGP, with USAID approval, reallocated budgeted funds to administer more grants. To date, nearly $15 million worth of grant-funded projects have been approved, and almost all are completed or nearing completion," he said.[326]

Statistically speaking, the $15 million was slightly less than 10 percent of the total $154 million paid out to RTI for the first year of work, which suggests that 90 percent was spent on company staff and administration expenses.

Kuhaida also complained that RTI lacked a serious plan for delivering democracy. "We can't even get our own people in the United States to vote, how are we going to do that in Iraq?" he wondered.

> We needed to at least do some strategizing and
> thinking, but I saw no evidence that we were doing
> that.... There was no plan at all after the war.... The
> whole thing was running on a whim, basically.
> There wasn't even a bad plan out there. I am total-
> ly disturbed by my government and the lies that
> were told to me. I take them personally.[327]

In response, Gibbons told me that the situation was
"challenging for everyone involved."

"Our efforts to date have been successful by any reasonable standard, and we are looking forward to continuing to
improve municipal government's service delivery, to ensure
that councils are representative, to promote the role of local
government in sovereign Iraq, and to promote public participation in national and local political processes," he said. "Is
it easy? No."

Not all the former employees who spoke with me blamed
RTI. Jim Beaulieu, a former deputy minister of urban affairs
in the Canadian province of Manitoba, was hired by RTI in
September 2003 to help the governor of Najaf, the highest-
ranked politician in the region.

Beaulieu said this work was more challenging than that
of the military contractor Bechtel, which was charged with
helping rebuild and protect Iraq's infrastructure. "RTI had to
deal with people, ordinary Iraqis, who had no fundamental
concept of democracy," he said. "We needed expatriates to
teach these concepts."

The problem, he believed, lay with the American occupation authorities in Baghdad, who had given the governor and
the governing council "no money, no authority over anything other than their own offices, and no support staff.

They were just a shell. They were trying hard to do things, but how can you do anything without money or authority?" Gibbons countered that the councils did have some power.

> It is not true that the roles and responsibilities of councils have been largely advisory during [the occupation]. Local councils across the country have been planning and developing priorities for their constituents and communities, and funding flows exceeding $2 million per province that are spent only on projects selected by the council have enabled councils to choose and then implement important projects. The system, of course, is not fully developed, but councils to date have played critical roles in conflict resolution, selecting governors/mayors, and implementing projects.[328]

But Gibbon's reassurances did little to assuage the men's concerns. By spring 2004, disenchanted with the company and frustrated by the little work being done, all three men quit their jobs and returned to North America. Beaulieu explained his motives thus: "I resigned because it became obvious we could not do what we were hired to do.... There was simply no credible evidence that the United States had a plan of what they want to do." Algarawi, too, was disenchanted with RTI. "They went there to make a profit, not to help the people," he said.

Gibbons says that the three men do not represent the views of all RTI staff.

> A lot of people have come out to Iraq to accomplish important personal missions.... Some have done

very well, and others have been daunted by the
complexity of the environment, the danger, or the
sheer frustration that even basic communications
among teams working on the same project could
not be taken for granted, that they had to be built
up from scratch by each of the contractors and the
CPA itself. In the face of these circumstances, some
have left earlier than they originally planned, in
frustration. Others have extended well beyond their
original commitment and feel they are accomplish-
ing critical tasks.[329]

CONCLUSION

SAIC's public work suggest that, at the very least, the company had bitten off more than it could chew. But then again,
if most of the company's work is classified, might one not
suspect that the secret work was being botched just as badly
as their failed public projects? Perhaps SAIC is not quite the
Big Brother that its eavesdropping contracts would suggest,
but more like so many other military contractors living
large off of contracts that it knows can never be publicly
audited. Maybe the much touted surveillance systems do
not work, which is why the spy agencies seem to have done
an awful job at tracking down threats to the United States.

Certainly there are many in the military and intelligence
community who believe that the excessive reliance on computer and satellite technology has hampered work and the
gleaning of good information, which they believe can only
be provided by human intelligence. In September 2001,
Jane's Defense Weekly commented, "One possible con-

tributing factor to this failure of the intelligence and security system could be the lack of resources the U.S. has devoted to human intelligence (HUMINT) capabilities throughout the past decade. While national technical means continued to receive high levels of funding for surveillance satellites, signals intelligence flights, and other eavesdropping technologies, human-based intelligence capabilities have withered."[330]

Should we hire psy-ops companies to run media networks? At the very least, one would expect that competent contractors, rather than firms with no experience, would be awarded contracts. Say what you will about the propagandistic nature of state media networks such as the Voice of America—at least they have listeners. And then there are state-funded media groups, the BBC and others, which are reasonably independent and boast very high listenerships.

For that matter should we use private contractors to plan an entire new government or design "democracy"? The IRDC employees I met were not really aware of SAIC, so they can be forgiven for being ignorant of the company's spy history. It has been argued that the SAIC contract existed to protect the individuals but through the Pentagon's role in the creation of the IRDC we now know that it also existed to promote the Pentagon's goals over those of the State Department, a dangerous and foolish interagency game to play when the future of a country and the fostering of true democracy is at stake.

Without true democracy, by choosing to rig or delay the system to allow "moderates" or "nonrejectionists" to win, the occupation authorities have dug their own grave. Iraqis no longer believe that the Americans intend to allow them to choose for themselves, with the exception, of course, of those who have benefited from the American system. This has in fact strenghtened rejectionists like Moqtada al Sadr— the very opposite of what the occupation authorities wanted to achieve in the first place. Whether RTI or SAIC are solely responsible for these failures is hard to say. After all, the "selection" system was ultimately approved by the U.S. military and government. These contractors are profiting handsomely from the process, but they should not entirely escape the burden of blame for Iraq's failing experiment in American export democracy.

Epilogue

On Monday, June 28, 2004, long before the sun had risen over the Potomac and while nightly television anchors and the American public slept, Paul Bremer, before a handful of specially invited guests deep inside occupation headquarters, issued a document transferring power to Sheikh Ghazi al-Yawar and Ayad Allawi, the two men appointed to take over the reins of government in Iraq. One hour later, Bremer was on board a helicopter, and a full hour before the first ray of light hit the dome of the U.S. capitol, a military aircraft was winging him back to the United States. The timing of this surprise clandestine ceremony allowed Bremer to make it for lunch at the White House on the official date of the transfer of power, June 30, 2004.

On the occasion of Bremer's departure the invited media received a stark picture of his exit: two Blackwater mercenaries watched his back, rifles pointed menacingly at camera crews, until Bremer boarded the aircraft and the cabin door closed. No flowers from an adoring Iraqi public, no "Mission Accomplished" banner on the deck of a warship, far less the dramatic lift-off from the roof of the U.S. embassy in Saigon marked the occasion, just a quiet, top-secret

escape to freedom (and a lucrative book contract). Baghdad
remained eerily silent for the next few days as the public at
large and the media both held their breath. Would there be
an explosion of violence? Would fundamentalist rebels seize
control of major Iraqi cities? No, the first week after
Bremer's departure proved a nonevent as far as the television
media was concerned.

Bremer's departure was only one in the exodus of occupation officials and contractors (an American soldier derisive-
ly called them the "League of Frightened Gentleman") who
were relieved to be out of immediate danger.[331] The German
engineers hired to repair the Daura power plant in Baghdad
fled in the last week of June leaving enormous disassembled
machines on the plant floor. ("They didn't contact me," said
Bashir Khalif Omir, the plant's director. "They took their
luggage at midnight and they left.")[332] Maybe some of them
had discovered how badly equipped the Iraqi police, now left
on their own, were. Less than 60 percent of the weapons
(141,000 of 253,000), a quarter of the body armor suits
(40,000 of 174,000), and 5 percent of the radios (2,500 of
57,000) that the police had ordered had been delivered, while
just over one-third of the requested vehicles (8,500 of 25,000)
had arrived by the time Bremer departed.[333] As scared foreign nationals fled the country, security threats could harm
no one but the locals.

Days after Iraq regained "sovereignty," the White House
revealed some startling details about the reconstruction:
just 2 percent of the $18.4 billion earmarked for the urgent
reconstruction of Iraq had been spent. Not a penny was
spent on healthcare or water and sanitation, two of the most
urgent needs for Iraqis.[334] Readers of this book, having
waded through the tales of waste and profiteering could be

confused: What is really going on—are we spending too much or too little money?

The answer lies in separating the apples from the pears and oranges. There are three treasure chests that the occupation authorities were allowed to dip their hands into; the $87 billion appropriation that Congress granted to the Bush administration in September 2003 was divided into two funds—$18.4 billion were earmarked for reconstruction and the bigger chunk, some $65 billion, was committed for military operations. The Development Fund of Iraq (a.k.a. the sale of Iraqi oil) forms the third fund.

Treasure chest number two was quickly spent hiring Halliburton to supply the soldiers. In fact, the military is now believed to have exceeded this allotment by an estimated $12 billion. This was the source of 90 percent of the money and of much of the criticism that the company received, the latter due to the careful audits of military investigators. The reconstruction money, treasure chest number one, was hardly touched because the bidding and oversight requirements were stringent to prevent fraud or waste. As a result, many of the reconstruction bills were paid for with revenue from the sale of Iraqi oil (treasure chest number three). Some of this money was spent hiring Halliburton for the repair of the oil infrastructure and some of it was simply handed out in cash by soldiers to local people in return for favors such as rebuilding offices or building football fields. A *New York Times* article published in late June 2004 described the lax oversight thus:

> The teams have become famous in Iraq for the way they have spread across the country, commissioning repairs and paying for them from satchels

bulging with $100 bills shipped by plane from a
Federal Reserve vault in East Rutherford, New
Jersey. At least $1 billion has been distributed in
this fashion—by some estimates more than $2 bil-
lion. "The military commanders love that program,
because it buys them friends," said an administration official, referring to the cash distribution. "You
want to hire everybody on the street, put money in
their pockets and make them like you. We have
always spent Iraqi money on that."[335]

In other words

1. U.S. taxpayers spent a lot of money on the soldiers, but
the Pentagon paid Halliburton to do the work and the latter
billed top dollar knowing the administration would look the
other way (until two brave members of Congress inquired
about the results of the internal audit);

2. Little of the money that American taxpayers provided
for reconstruction was spent, because the rules were so com-
plicated; and

3. We dished out Iraqi money like it was going out of
style, because the United States government knew that neither Congress nor the United Nations would ask us difficult
questions.

With all this talk of gouging and profiteering, I've been
asked why I've not addressed oil in more detail. After all,
wasn't this a war about oil? And what about the infamous
no-bid contracts, Dick Cheney's role in awarding contracts,
and the wholesale privatization of Iraq's state industries?

Put simply, this book chronicles what happened in the
first year of liberation as I and other journalists in Iraq and
Washington, D.C. experienced it. For a discussion of foreign

policy and the ideology behind the invasion you will have to look to more experienced analysts than myself. I do believe that the war took place for two reasons: to distract the public's attention from the Bush administration's failure to rebuild crumbling domestic infrastructure—schools, hospitals, and social security—and to strengthen the U.S. military presence in the Middle East. Oil was a factor in the invasion, but also proved incidental to that action. After all, the United States was one of the biggest buyers of Iraqi oil before the war and still is after the war. Whether or not the lucrative new oil concessions will be given to the Russians, the French, or the Americans is still a matter of speculation, and this book has attempted only to deal in facts, that is, what happened on the ground. In fact, Halliburton does not control the oil wells nor hold any oil concessions. It is simply an oil services company, providing expertise to oil companies who own such concessions. The bigger, somewhat less conspiratorial, question regards its military contracts in Iraq, worth ten times those of its contracts in the oil sector.

As far as no-bid contracts are concerned, most of the contracts (such as the Bechtel reconstruction contract) were won in limited competition, with the exceptions of the oil-fire dousing contract and the Iraqi Media Network contract, both of which were awarded without bidding. Had these contracts been openly bid upon, would Halliburton or SAIC have won them? SAIC's qualifications for the IMN contract were lacking, but Halliburton is one of the biggest and most experienced companies in the business at providing overall logistical support to the military, such that they hold a de facto monopoly. And despite the fact that many Iraqis are perfectly qualified to cook food and drive trucks, they will never get these jobs because the military is afraid of hiring

locals and Iraqi companies cannot meet the bidding requirements dictated by Washington, D.C. Ironically, the
American companies simply turn around and hire local
companies to perform the menial labor, while the executives in Washington D.C., Houston, and San Francisco
receive a fat finder's fee.

Did the occupation authorities pick the wrong companies? Clearly, SAIC had no experience in nation-building;
Vinnell was a failure at building an army; and the Dyncorp
trainers were too trigger happy to notice that they were contributing to a rising Iraqi anger while unknowingly providing a cover for the resistance. The Bearing Point experiments
with privatization were a disaster, and the RTI model city
councils were teaching Iraqis that America was not interested in empowering them but in building up a pliant local government, dependent on American handouts. Bechtel's failure to fix the infrastructure in twelve months, however
understandable, did not help mollify Iraqis who were already
hearing rumors of torture and death at the hands of
American soldiers and mysterious civilians in the Abu
Ghraib prison and elsewhere. While thousands clamored for
jobs with Halliburton, many more were convinced that the
company was stealing Iraqi oil.

Will we ever know if Frank Dall, Janet Ballantyne, and
Dick Cheney pulled strings to win those lucrative contracts
in Iraq? Will we ever discover why CACI's contracts were
signed in Sierra Vista, Arizona, instead of in Washington or
Baghdad, and issued by the Department of the Interior
instead of the Pentagon? Would the American taxpayer and
the Iraqi citizen, both, have been better served had we done
our homework, held a free and fair competition, or picked a
different company? Certainly had we spent more of Iraq's oil

revenues on directly hiring Iraqi companies and workers, we might have quelled some of the anger gathering among the millions of unemployed men on the streets of Basra, Kirkuk, and Baghdad. It is that anger that threatens to undo all the work that has been done so far.

Who should be rebuilding Iraq? I think the answer is simple, although not necessarily easy to implement. Iraqis need to be in charge of the process. Iraqi companies need to be awarded the contracts and Iraqi workers should get first crack at jobs. Does that mean that foreign companies should be excluded from the process? Not at all, especially when they have an expertise that might not be available locally. Iraq has always hired foreign experts to oversee the building and maintenenence of its power plants and no doubt that they will want to hire companies like Halliburton to help them with sophisticated oil drilling equipment, as does almost every oil company in the world. But these decisions need to be made by Iraqis, not Americans, in Baghdad not Washington D.C., and the process needs to be as open and transparent as possible, with payments made conditional on delivering working services on time.

Under such rules, taxpayer dollars will be better spent and fly-by-night companies will not apply for jobs they cannot complete. Contracts to deliver public services such as education and health should be delivered by nonprofits or international institutions with a track record, while "democracy" contracts should be canceled if they amount to an attempt to interfere in the affairs of a sovereign people.

This brings us to the toughest question of all: Who should make these decisions in Iraq—a "selected" government with shadowy American advisors or a truly democratic elected government? As I write these final words in late July 2004, fifteen months after the invasion was complete, it boggles the mind that a system of voting was not the first priority and still is not the most important item on the U.S. agenda. With confidence in the new government ebbing by the day and violence on all sides rising—the American troops renewing attacks on Falluja, and hostage taking, killings and suicide bombings increasing (two of the eighteen governors of Iraq were assassinated in July 2004 alone)—this needs to be the biggest priority. Yet, given legitimate elections and the quick withdrawal of the troops, will Iraqis pick the "right" government? Will there be a bloodbath? Will they vote in Saddam's old henchmen or Islamic fundamentalists? No one knows. But on the issue of democracy, American style, the citizens of sovereign Iraq are unequivocal.

NOTES

----

1. Interviews and notes by author, 9 April 2004.
2. Richard Lezin Jones and Jill Capuzzo, "U.S. Officials Failed to Protect Slain Civilian, Family Says," *The New York Times*, 13 May 2004.
3. Paul Bremer, Remarks to Governing Council, Baghdad City Council, 24 March 2004, posted on the Web at http://www.iraqcoalition.org/transcripts/20040324 Bremer 100.html.
4. Jonathan Weisman and Ariana Eunjung Cha, "Rebuilding Aid Unspent, Tapped to Pay Expenses," *Washington Post*, 30 April 2004.
5. Ibid.
6. Matt Kelley, "Fewer Than 25,000 Iraqis Working on Reconstruction Funded by US," Associated Press, 18 May 2004.
7. Jim Garamone, "Coalition Encouraging Private Business Growth in Iraq," *American Forces Press Service*, 18 February 2004.
8. "Iraq's Army of Unemployed," *CBSnews.com*, 16 October 2003. http://www.cbsnews.com/stories/2003/10/17/iraq/main578544.shtml.
9. Kelley, op. cit.
10. Ewa Jasiewicz, interviewed by author, 13 December 2003.
11. David Bacon, "US Arrests Iraq's Union Leaders," *Pacific News Service*, 10 December 2003.
12. Russell Gold, "The Temps of War: Blue-Collar Workers Ship Out For Iraq," *Wall Street Journal*, 25 February 2003.
13. *NBC News*, 12 December 2003. "Contractor Served Troops Dirty Food in Dirty Kitchens," *Agence France Press*, 14 December 2003.
14. Ibid.
15. Neil King, "Halliburton Hits Snafu on Billing in Kuwait," *Wall Street Journal*, 2 February 2003.
16. Gold, op. cit.
17. Melissa Norcross, email to author, 9 February 2004.

18. David Rohd, "Exploited in Iraq, Indian Workers Say," *The New York Times*, 7 May 2004.

19. Nick Grim, "Queensland Company Loses Lucrative Iraq Contract," *The World Today*, 21 May 2004.

20. Marian Wilkinson, "Corruption Stench as Company Loses Iraq Contract," *Sydney Morning Herald*, 21 May 2004.

21. Testimony of Henry Bunting, "Senate Democratic Policy Committee Oversight Hearing on Iraq Reconstruction Contracts," 13 February 2004.

22. Ibid.

23. David Ivanovich, "Halliburton Questioning Focuses on Towels' Cost," *Houston Chronicle*, 14 February 2004.23.

24. Bunting, op. cit.

25. Robert Michael West, statement, 6 June 2004, posted on the Web site of the Committee on Government Reform Minority Committee at http://www.house.gov/reform/min/inves_admin/ admin_contracts.htm.

26. Russell Gold, "Halliburton Unit Runs into Big Obstacles in Iraq," *Wall Street Journal*, 28 April 2004.

27. Ibid.

28. David Wilson, statement, 13 June 2004, posted on the Web site of the Committee on Government Reform Minority Committee at http://www.house.gov/reform/min/inves_admin/admin_contracts.htm.

29. Seth Borenstein, "Trucks Made to Drive without Cargo in Dangerous Areas of Iraq," *Knight Ridder*, 21 May 2004.

30. Jeffrey Rodengen, *The Legend of Halliburton* (Fort Lauderdale: Write Stuff Press, 1996).

31. Linda Gillan, "Brown & Root is a Golden Problem Child for Halliburton," *Houston Chronicle*, 4 March 1980.

32. Oliver Burkeman, "Cheney Firm Paid Millions in Bribes to Nigerian Official," *Guardian*, 9 May 2003.

33. Rodengen, op. cit., p. 72

34. Robert Caro, *The Years of Lyndon Johnson: The Path To Power*, (New York: Alfred Knopf, 1982).

35. Dan Briody, *The Halliburton Agenda* (New York: Wiley, 2004), p. 165.

36. Raymond Klempin, *Houston Business Journal*, 13 September 1982, p. 133.

37. Al Kamen, "Unearthing Democratic Root to Halliburton Flap," *Washington Post*, 5 March 2004.

38. Bill Hartung and Frida Berrigan, "Is What's Good for Boeing and Halliburton Good for America?" *World Policy Institute*, February 2004.

39. Pentagon biography of Richard B. Cheney posted at http://www.defenselink.mil/specials/secdef_histories/bios/cheney.htm.

40. Jane Mayer, "Contract Sport," *New Yorker*, 10 February 2004.

41. "Somalis Protest Dismissals by a U.S. Company," Reuters, 5 November 1994.

42. Richard B. Cheney's resume posted at http://www.whitehouse.gov/vicepresident/; Knut Royce and Nathaniel Heller, "Cheney Led Halliburton To Feast at Federal Trough," August 2, 2001, posted on the Center for Public Integrity Web site at http://www.public-i.org/dtaweb/report.asp?ReportID=172&L1=10&L2=70&L3=15&L4=0&

L5=0; "Loyal and Experienced: Cheney a Washington Insider with a Long Political Resume," posted on the CNN Web site at http://www.cnn.com/SPECIALS/2000/democracy/bush/stories/cheney/ ; Katherine Pfleger, "US Embassies Assisted Cheney Firm," Associated Press, 26 October 2000; and Robert Bryce, "Cheney's Multi-Million Dollar Revolving Door," Mother Jones, 2 August 2000.

43.   "Cheney May Still Have Halliburton Ties," CNN, 25 September 2003, and Vice President Dick Cheney and Mrs. Cheney Release 2003 Income Tax Return, Office of the Vice President, 10 April 2004.

44.   Mary Williams Walsh, "Shriveling of Pensions After Halliburton Deal," The New York Times, 10 September 2002.

45.   DickCheney, interviewed by Tim Russert, Meet the Press, NBC, 14 September 2003.

46.   Business Industry Political Action Committee, "Project 2000," "Where Do We Go From Here?" and "Prosperity Project," posted at http://www.bipac.org/home.asp.

47.   Halliburton, "Former Four-Star General Flag Officer Admiral 'Joe' Lopez Joins Halliburton Business Unit", press release, 20 July 1999.

48.   Mike Noll, interview by author, May 2002.

49.   Bob Whistine, "Tent Cities Spring Up Across Kuwait," Army News Service, 25 February 2003.

50.   Dan Baum, "Nation Builders for Hire," The New York Times Magazine, 22 June 2003.

51.   Whistine, op. cit.

52.   Author visit to Adana and Ayla Jean Yackley, "US Pilots Prowl Skies Over Northern Iraq," Reuters, 25 January 2002.

53.   Major Toni Kemper, interview by Sasha Lilley of CorpWatch, January 2003.

54.   David Ivanovich, "Obstacles Are Many on Iraq's Oil Fields," Houston Chronicle, 29 April 2003.

55.   Baum, op. cit.

56.   Peter S. Goodman, "Iraq: At Oil Plant, Bitterness and Idleness," Washington Post, 30 April 2003.

57.   Don Van Natta Jr., "High Payments to Halliburton for Fuel in Iraq," The New York Times, 10 December 2003.

58.   Chip Cummins, "US Officials May Have Steered Halliburton to Kuwaiti Supplier," Wall Street Journal, 15 December 2003.

59.   Neil King Jr., "Halliburton Tells Pentagon Workers Took Kickbacks to Award Projects in Iraq," Wall Street Journal, 23 January 2004.

60.   T. Christian Miller, "Contract Flaws in Iraq Cited," Los Angeles Times, 11 March 2004.

61.   "Pentagon Was Warned in 2002 of Contractors," Associated Press, 7 May 2004.

62.   Eric Rosenberg, "Despite Warnings, KBR Got Contract," Hearst News Service, 15 May 2004.

63.   Gold, op. cit.

64.   Russell Gold and Christopher Cooper, "Pentagon Weighs Criminal Charges of Halliburton Arm," Wall Street Journal, 23 January 2004.

65. Greg Jaffe and Neil King Jr., "US General Criticizes Halliburton," *Wall Street Journal*, 15 March 2004.

66. Sue Pleming, "US Questions More Halliburton Bills," Reuters, 17 May 2004.

67. Marie de Young, statement, 6 June 2004, posted on the Web site of the Committee on Government Reform Minority Committee, at http://www.house.gov/reform/min/inves_admin/admin_contracts.htm.

68. Mayer, op. cit.

69. Jackie Spinner and Mary Pat Flaherty, "Iraq: Rebuilding Plan Reviewed," *Washington Post*, 31 March 2004.

70. Posted on the Web at http://swz.salary.com/

71. Hartung and Berrigan, op.cit.

72. Yaruub Jasim, interview by author, 14 December 2003.

73. Jeff Berger, Bechtel press office, email to author, 10 January 2004.

74. Douglas Jehl, "Pentagon Bars Three Nations From Iraq Bids," *The New York Times*, 10 December 2003.

75. David Baker, "Bechtel Under Siege: Iraqis Seethe as Sabotage, Red Tape Slow Repair Effort," *San Francisco Chronicle*, 21 September 2003.

76. Ibid.

77. USAID, "Local USAID Awards Iraq Infrastructure II Contract," press release, 6 January 2004, and USAID, "Local USAID Awards Iraq Infrastructure Contract," press release, 17 April 2003.

78. Richard Oppel Jr. with Diana Henriques, "Bechtel Has Ties in Washington, and to Iraq," *The New York Times*, 17 April 2003.

79. Posted on the Bechtel Web site at http://www.bechtel.com/default_about.htm.

80. David Baker, "US: Bechtel's 2003 Revenue Breaks Company Record," *San Francisco Chronicle*, 20 April 2004.

81. Dan Baum, interview by author, July 2004.

82. George Shultz, "Act Now.The Danger Is Immediate: Saddam Hussein Must Be Removed," *Washington Post*, 6 September 2002.

83. Jim Vallette with Steve Kretzmann and Daphne Wysham, "Crude Vision," *Institute for Policy Studies*, March 2003.

84. Posted on the OPIC Web site at http://www.opic.gov/staff/Exec/BIO-Connelly.htm; ExIm, "ExIm Bank 2003 Advisory Committee Convenes First Meeting," press release, 25 March 2003; and André Verlöy and Daniel Politi, "Focus on Key Industry Sectors, Advisor Ties to Defense Contractors," *The Center for Public Integrity*, 29 March 2003.

85. Steve LeBlanc, "Natsios: 'It's a New Day for the Big Dig,'" Associated Press, 12 April 2000.

86. Juliette Beck, interview by author, April 2003.

87. Jimmy Langman, "Bechtel Battles Against Dirt-Poor Bolivia," *San Francisco Chronicle*, 2 February 2002.

88. Posted on the *Boston Globe* Web site at http://www.boston.com/globe/metro/bigdig/.

89. Roger Moody, "The Gulliver," *Minewatch*, 1992; and Don May, president of California Earth Corp, interview by author, May 2000.

90. Aviva Imhof, "The Big, Ugly Australian Goes to Ok Tedi," *Multinational Monitor*, March 1996.

91. Center for Responsive Politics, "Rebuilding Iraq —The Contractors," 28 April 2003, posted at http://www.opensecrets.org/news/rebuilding_iraq/index.asp.

92. Ted Morris, interview by author, 11 December 2003.

93. David Bacon, "Umm Qasr: From National Pride to War Booty," *CorpWatch*, 15 December 2003.

94. Bacon, op.cit.

95. Bacon, op.cit.

96. Bacon, op.cit.

97. Rod Nordland and Michael Hirsh, "US: The $87 Billion Money Pit," *Newsweek*, 27 October 2003.

98. Colin Rowat, "How the Sanctions Hurt Iraq," *Middle East Report and Information Project*, delivered at Global Policy Forum, 2 August 2001.

99. Mohsen Hassan, interview by author, 7 December 2003.

100. Larry Kaplow, "US: Bechtel Criticized Over School Project in Iraq," *Palm Beach Post-Cox News Service*, 14 December 2003.

101. Nordland and Hirsh, op.cit.

102. Karim El-Gawhary, "Selling Success to the Arabs," *Al-Ahram Weekly*, 20–26 November 2003.

103. Francis Canavan and Jonathan Marshall, interviews by author, April and May 2004.

104. Sa'ad Mohammed, interview by author, December 2004.

105. Translator, interview by author, 18 April 2004.

106. "Bechtel's Dry Run," *Public Citizen*, April 2004.

107. Ibid.

108. Canavan interview, op. cit.

109. Jackie Spinner, "Operation Iraqi Education," *Washington Post*, 21 April 2003.

110. Jackie Spinner, "Questions Raised About Creative Associates Contract," *Washington Post*, 13 June 2003.

111. Center for Public Integrity, "Profile of Creative Associates," *Windfalls of War*, posted at http://www.publici.org/wow/bio.aspx?act=pro&ddlC=11.

112. Justin Huggler, "Dying of Neglect: The State of Iraq's Children's Hospitals," *The Independent*, 21 February 2004, and Jeffrey Gettleman, "Chaos and War Leave Iraq's Hospitals in Ruins," *The New York Times*, 14 February 2004.

113. Dr. Haqqi I Razzaouki, interview by author, 19 April 2004.

114. Gettleman, op.cit.

115. Paul Martin, "U.S. Aims to Lower Iraqi Child Death Rate," *Washington Times*, 21 June 2003.

116. Ammar al Saffar, interview by author, 7 April 2004.

117. Gettleman, op. cit.

118. David Baker, "SF Firm Awarded Contract in Iraq," *San Francisco Chronicle*, 12 March 2004.

119. Posted on the Web at http://www.abtassoc.com/.

120. Hospital director, interview by author, 14 December 2003.

121. USAID, "Iraqi Nursing Association Receives US Grant," press release, 21 July 2003 and USAID, "US Government Assistance to Iraqi Health Services," press release, 28 July 2003.
122. Center for Public Integrity, "Profile of Abt Associates," *Windfalls of War*, posted at http://www.publicintegrity.org/wow/bio.aspx?act=pro&ddlC=1.
123. Saffar interview, op. cit.
124. Yarub al-Shiraida, interview by author, 14 April 2004.
125. Hassan Rawi, interview by author, 14 April 2004.
126. Dr. Koresh al Qaseer, interview by author, 15 April 2004.
127. Haitham Haddadin, "Trade Bank of Iraq Gets $2.4 Billion Export Guarantees," Reuters, 24 January 2004.
128. Mitch Jeserich, "Banking on Empire," *CorpWatch*, 4 February 2004. Posted at htp://corpwatch.org/article.php?id=9848.
129. Crispian Balmer, "Rome Accord on Iraqi Loans Set to Help Trade," Reuters, 5 December 2003.
130. Posted on the Web site of the Center for Public Integrity at http://www.public-i.org/bop2004/candidate.aspx?cid=2&act=cp.
131. Greg Cresci, "J. P. Morgan, Bank One Announce Board Slate," Reuters, 3 May 2003.
132. Jeserich, op.cit.
133. Insurance Firms Issued Slave Policies: Various Documents Link Modern Companies to Antebellum Slavery, James Cox, *USA Today*, 21 February 2002.
134. U.S. National Archives & Records Administration, *Thousands of Intelligence Documents Opened under the Nazi War Crimes*, 13 May 2004.
135. Khulumani et al., statement by Cohen, Milstein, Hausfeld & Toll, 12 November 2002.
136. University of California, "Banks, Law Firms Were Pivotal in Executing Enron Securities Fraud," press release, 8 April 2002.
137. Sandhya D'mello, "IFC Plans to Venture into Iraq by June," *Khaleej Times*, 14 March 2004.
138. Adrian Gatton and Clayton Hirst, "A Booty for the Barons of Baghdad," *The Independent*, 8 February 2004.
139. Laura Rozen, "Strange Bedfellows: U.S. Contractor in Iraq Helped Fund Al Qaeda," *The Nation*, 25 October 2003.
140. David Baker, "Short Iraqi Road Is Feat for Bechtel: Bypass Is First Completed Project in War-Torn Country," *San Francisco Chronicle*, 22 July 2003.
141. Iraq Revenue Watch, "Controlling Iraq's Skies: The Secret Sell-off of Iraq's Air Industry," Open Society Institute, March 2004.
142. Posted on the Kubba Web site at http://www.kubba-group.com/
143. Gatton and Hirst, op. cit.
144. Roula Khalaf, "Support for Radical Iraqi Cleric Surging, Poll Shows," *Financial Times*, 20 May 2004.
145. Man Bahadur Gurung, interview by author, 8 December 2003.
146. Maniram Gurung, interview by author, 3 December 2003.
147. Mohammed al-Husany, interview by author, 3 December 2003.

148. Security guards, interview by author, 2 April 2004.
149. Viewed by author, 14 December 2003.
150. Colin Freeman, "UK Security Guard Killed in Iraq," *The Scotsman*, 29 March 2004.
151. "Job Scarcity Forcing Ex-Servicemen To Work As Mercenaries In Iraq," *The Hindu*, 6 April 2004.
152. "Ratendra's Life Mission," *Sunday People*, 14 September 2003.
153. Christian Jennings, "Special Forces Quitting to Cash in on Iraq," *The Scotsman*, 21 February 2004.
154. Eric Schmitt, "Plans Made for Policing Iraq," *The New York Times*, 9 April 2003.
155. Homer Newman, interview by author, 7 April 2003.
156. Chuck Wilkins, interview by author, 7 April 2003.
157. Coalition Provisional Authority, *Executive Agency Discussion of Selection*, Web site, 17 April 2003. Posted at http://iraqcoalition.org/economy/PMO/Executive_Agency_Discussion.htm.
158. Mark Fineman, "Privatized Army in Harm's Way," *Los Angeles Times*, 24 January 2003.
159. Dan Baum, "This Gun For Hire," *Wired*, February 2003.
160. Computer Sciences Corporation, "Computer Sciences Corporation Completes Acquisition Of Dyncorp," press release, 7 March 2003.
161. Baum, op. cit.
162. Baum, op. cit.
163. Kelly Patricia O'Meara, "Dyncorp Disgrace," *Insight*, 14 January 2002.
164. Tucker Carlson, "Hired Guns," *Esquire*, March 2004.
165. Ibid.
166. Paul Dykes, "Desert Storm: How Did a Convicted Ulster Terror Squaddie Get Security Job in Iraq?" *Belfast Telegraph*, 5 February 2004.
167. Carlson, op. cit.
168. Roy Wenzl, "Two Wichitans See Iraqi Chaos Surge," *The Wichita Eagle*, 15 April 2004.
169. E-mail correspondence on Private Military Contractor list-serv run by International Peace Operations Association.
170. Dathar al-Kashab, interview by author, 8 December 2003.
171. Mamand Kesnazani, interview by author, 3 April 2003.
172. Aaron Glantz, "Mercenary Boom in Iraq Creates Tension at Home and Abroad," *CorpWatch*, 23 March 2004. Available on the CorpWatch Web site at http://ww.corpwatch.org/article.php?id=10288.
173. *WACAM Fact-Finding Mission to the Wassa West District of Ghana's Western Region in 1999*, posted on the WACAM Web site at http://www.nodirtygold.org/sansu_ghana.cfm.
174. Graeme Hosken, Elize Jacobs and Tracy Lee Goldstone, "Pretoria Man Killed in Iraq," *Pretoria News*, 29 January 2004, and Beauregard Tromp, "South African Hired Guns Flock to Iraq," *The Star*, 4 February 2004.
175. Julian Rademeyer, "Vlakplaas Henchman Injured in Iraq," *Sunday Times*, 21 March 2004.
176. Julian Rademeyer, "Iraq Victim Was Top-Secret Apartheid Killer," *Sunday Times*, 18 April 2004.

177. "Lucrative Pay Lures Cream of SA Cops to Iraq," *Sunday Independent*, 8 February 2004.
178. Knut Royce, "Start-up Company with Connections," *Newsday*, 15 February 2004.
179. Matt Moore, "Insurgents Posing as Police Kill 2 Americans," Associated Press, 11 March 2004.
180. Coalition Press Information Center, "Fourth Infantry Division Soldiers Repel Automatic Weapons Attack," press release, 8 February 2004.
181. Ariana Eunjung Cha, "Recruits Abandon New Iraqi Army," *Washington Post*, 13 December 2003.
182. Ibid.
183. "Vinnell Adds Saudis To Its Trainee Roster," *Business Week*, 24 February 1975.
184. Kim Willenson, Nicholas Profitt, and Lloyd Norman, "Saudi Arabia: This Gun For Hire," *Newsweek*, 24 February 1975.
185. John Burns, "Pool Report on Ambassador Bremer's Trip to Mosul," *The New York Times*,1 April 2004, and James Dao, "Corporate Security Goes to the Front Line, *The New York Times*, 2 April 2004.
186. Kirsten Scharnberg and Mike Dorning, "Iraq Violence Drives Thriving Business," *Chicago Tribune*, 2 April 2004, and Barry Yeoman, "Soldiers of Good Fortune," *Mother Jones*, May/June 2003.
187. Jaymes Song, "Civilian Deaths Spark Grief, Outrage in Hawaii," Associated Press, 3 April 2004.
188. Rod Nordland, "The Iraqi Intifada," *Newsweek* (web exclusive), 12 April 2004. Posted at http://msnbc.msn.com/id/4710176.
189. Jonathan Franklin, "U.S. Contractor Recruits Guards for Iraq in Chile," *Guardian*, 5 March 2004.
190. Dana Priest, "Private Guards Repel Attack on U.S. Headquarters," *Washington Post*, 6 April 2004.
191. Edward Wong, "Iraqi Militias Resisting US Pressure to Disband," *The New York Times*, 9 February 2004.
192. Nicholas Pelham, "Rival Former Exile Groups Clash Over Security in Iraq," *Financial Times*, 12 December 2003.
193. Wong, op.cit.
194. Dana Priest and Mary Pat Flaherty, "Security Firms Form World's Largest Private 'Army,'" *Washington Post*, 8 April 2004.
195. John Hooper and Nick Paton Walsh, "Video Reveals Full Horror of Italian Hostage's Execution," *Guardian*, 15 April 2004.
196. "Romanian Firm Pulls Out of Iraq After Attack," Reuters, 21 April 2004.
197. Major Gary Tallman, interview by author, 7 June 2004.
198. Lieutenant Colonel Alan Browne, interview by author, 7 June 2004.
199. Posted on the GAO Web site at http://www.gao.gov/decision/docket/ (File Number: B-294232.001).
200. Peter Singer, "Nation Builders and Low Bidders in Iraq," *The New York Times*, 15 June 2004.
201. Doug Brooks, interview by author, 3 June 2004.
202. Tim Spicer, *An Unorthodox Soldier*, (Vermont: Trafalgar Square, 2000).

203. Mary-Louise O'Callaghan, *Enemies Within, Papua New Guinea, Australia, and the Sandline Crisis: The Inside Story*, (Sydney: Doubleday, 1999).
204. David Isenberg, interview by author, May 2004.
205. Jon Dougherty, "Army to Cut Funding for Intelligence School?"*WorldNetDaily.com,* 30 January 2002. Posted at http://worldnet-daily.com/news/article.asp?ARTICLE_ID=26243.
206. Company history on CACI Web site, at http://www.caci.com/about/his tory/timeline.htm.
207. CACI, "CACI Wins Mission Support Contract with Air Force Materiel Command," press release, 23 January 1997.
208. "CACI At A Glance," *CACI Investor Update,* February 2004.
209. "CACI Directors and Senior Officers," posted on the CACI Web site at http://www.caci.com/about/management.shtml.
210. CACI Job Database. Posted on the CACI Web site at http://cacirecruit-ing.caci.com/jobpostings.nsf/949b67190f4be56a85256ccc005ce91c/2027c c36af1a5b8185256e9300607add?OpenDocument.
211. Scott Shane, "The Interrogators," *Baltimore Sun,* 7 May 2004.
212. Titan, "Titan Wins Share of $3B Communications and Technology Contract," press release, 17 September 2002.
213. Titan, "The U.S. Army and Titan Systems Corporation Announce Roll Out Of Prophet Block I, Delivery Exactly 365 Days after Contract Awarded," press release, 12 June 2002.
214. Titan, "Titan Wins $54.8 Million Air Force Electronic Systems Center AWACS Support Contract," press release, 14 January 2003.
215. Titan, "Titan Wins $18 Million Navy Wargaming Contract," press release, 27 December 2001.
216. Ronald D. White, "For Titan, Deaths Hit Close to Home," *Los Angeles Times,* 19 April 2004; Afghaniyat Yahoo Group listserv, July 11, 2002, posted at http://groups.yahoo.com/group/afghaniyat/message/3073; and a message posted on the Web site of *Barzan,* a Kurdish newspaper at http://www.barzan.com/upcoming_events35.html.
217. Afghaniyat, op.cit.
218. White, op. cit.
219. "US seeking Nashville Kurds," Associated Press, 12 December 2003.
220. White, op. cit.
221. Matthew Hay Brown, "Civilian Vetting Poses Obstacle For Military, Suspected Spying Raises Issues Of Private Contractors' Screening," *Orlando Sentinel,* 12 October 2003.
222. Katherine Pfleger Shrader, "CIA Sought Contractors for Interrogators," Associated Press, 12 May 2004.
223. Colin Freeman, "Iraq: Bay Area Civilian Vanishes in Iraq," *San Francisco Chronicle,* 11 November 2003.
224. Bradley J. Fikes, "Kuwait: Poway Man Killed, San Diegan Injured," *North County Times,* 22 January 2003.
225. Tony Capaccio, "Titan Payments Withheld Over Iraq Billing Dispute," *Bloomberg.com,* 12 March 2004.
226. Interview with the source by author, 6 May 2004.

227. Andy Pasztor and Jonathan Karp, "Titan Foreign Payments Scrutinized," *Wall Street Journal*, 22 March 2004.

228. "Wall Street Analysts Approve Of Revised Lockheed-Titan Merger Agreement," *InsideDefense.com*, 8 April 2004.

229. Renae Merle, "U.S. Opens Probe Into Contractor Titan Corp: Bribery Allegations Could Derail Buyout Deal by Lockheed," *Washington Post*, 6 March 2004.

230. Pasztor and Karp, op. cit.

231. Shane Harris, interview by author, October 2003.

232. Shane Harris, "Pentagon Mental Health Contract May Have Been Written by Vendors," *Government Executive*, 30 October 2003.

233. Major General Antonio M. Taguba, "Article 15-6 Investigation of the 800th Military Police Brigade," Department of Defense, February 2004.Posted at http://www.corpwatch.org/upload/document/taguba.pdf.

234. Douglas Jehl and Eric Schmitt, "Dogs and Other Harsh Tactics Linked to Military Intelligence," *The New York Times*, 22 May 2004.

235. Joel Brinkley, "U.S. Civilian Working at Abu Ghraib Disputes Army's Version of His Role in Abuses," *The New York Times*, 26 May 2004.

236. Julian Borger, "Cooks and Drivers Were Working as Interrogators," *Guardian*, 7 May 2004.

237. David Leigh, "Who Commands the Private Soldiers?" *Guardian*, 17 May 2004.

238. Jehl and Schmitt, op. cit.

239. Brinkley, op. cit.; Robert Tanner, "Civilians in Prison Scandal Raise Issues," Associated Press, 22 May 2004; and Matt Kelley, "Civilian Interpreter at Abu Ghraib Fired," Associated Press, 23 May 2004.

240. Joel Brinkley, "Translator Questioned by Army in Iraq Abuse," *The New York Times*, 12 May 2004.

241. William Lawson, interview by author, 1 May 2004.

242. CACI, "CACI Responds to Allegations in the Media About Its Employees in Iraq and to Financial Community Interests," press release, 5 May 2004.

243. Adam Liptak, "Who Would Try Civilians of U.S.? No One in Iraq," *The New York Times*, 26 May 2004.

244. Scott Shane, "Some U.S. Prison Contractors May Avoid Charges," *Baltimore Sun*, 24 May 2004.

245. Joel Brinkley, "200,000 Employees Awaiting Clearance to Work for Military," *The New York Times*, 12 May 2004.

246. Ken Silverstein, *Private Warriors*, (New York: Verso, 2000).

247. Lolita Baldor, "Senators Seek Investigation Into Private Security Firms in Iraq," Associated Press, 29 April 2004.

248. Douglas Jehl with Jane Prelez, "U.S. Installing Exiles in Key Positions," *The New York Times*, 26 April 2003.

249. United States Department of Defense, "DoD Announces Top Contractors for Fiscal Year 2004," press release no. 098-04, 11 February 2004.

250. Paul Kaihla, "In the Company of Spies," *Business 2.0*, May 2003.

251. SAIC, "SAIC Ranks in Top 300 Highest Revenue Businesses," posted at http://www.saic.com/cover-archive/saicachieve/500.html. and SAIC Annual Report, 2003, http://www.saic.com/news/annual.html.

252. Kaihla, op. cit.

253. Kaihla, op. cit.

254. Bechtel, "SAIC Combine to Win DoE Contract," press release, 14 November 2000; Scott Shane, "Uncle Sam Keeps SAIC On Call For Top Tasks," *Baltimore Sun*, 26 October 2003; and Bonnie Azab, "Why Aren't They Public? A Company Tom Clancy Would Love," *Corporate Board Member*, Sept/Oct 2002.

255. Shane, op. cit.

256. Zainab Abdul Hameed, interview by author, December 2003.

257. Bruce V. Bigelow, "Report Rips SAIC Over Iraq Contracts," *San Diego Union-Tribune*, 25 March 2004.

258. Jeanine Herbst, "SAIC to Stand Watch Over Athens Olympics," *Washington Business Journal*, 22 May 2003.

259. SAIC, "National Security. Information Dominance/Command and Control," posted on the SAIC Web site at http://www.saic.com/natsec/dominance.html.

260. Katrin Dauenhauer and Jim Lobe, "Middle East: Military Contractor's Media Mess," *Inter Press Service*, 16 August 2003.

261. Don North, "Iraq: Project Frustration, One Newsman's Take on How Things Went Wrong," *Television Week*, 15 December 2003.

262. Kathleen McCaul, "The Iraqi Media Network," *Baghdad Bulletin*, 21 July 2003.

263. Ibid.

264. Alaa Fa'ik, interview by author, December 2003.

265. Bigelow, op. cit.

266. Walter Pincus, "U.S. Firm to Run Iraqi TV, Harris Corp. Also to Operate National Newspaper," *Washington Post*, 12 January 2004.

267. Ibid.

268. Nancy Snow, "Al Hurra-Al Who? Haven't Heard? We're Free, They're Not!" *O'Dwyer's PR Daily*, 9 March 2004.

269. Al-Khafaji, interview author, April 2004.

270. Douglas Jehl, "U.S.-Backed Iraqi Exiles Return to Reinvent Nation," *The New York Times*, 4 May 2003.

271. IRDC members, interviews by author, December 2003 and April 2004.

272. Jehl, op. cit.

273. Jehl and Perlez. op. cit.

274. Al-Khafaji interview, op. cit.

275. Wendy Ross, "Bush Meets with Iraqis Who Have Fled Saddam Hussein," *Washington File*, 4 April 2003.

276. Jehl, op. cit.

277. Jehl, op. cit. and IRDC member interviews, op. cit.

278. Jonathan S. Landay and Warren P. Strobel, "Pentagon Civilians' Lack of Planning Contributed to Chaos in Iraq," *Knight Ridder*, 12 July 2003.

279. Jehl, op. cit.

280. Isam al-Khafaji, "I Did Not Want to be a Collaborator," *Guardian*, 28 July 2003.

281. Neil King Jr., "Bush Officials Devise a Broad Plan For Free-Market Economy in Iraq," *Wall Street Journal*, 1 May 2003.

282. General Jay Garner, interview with Greg Palast, BBC *NewsNight*, 22 March 2004.
283. "President Appoints Greenwich Man to Iraq Position," Associated Press, 7 August 2003.
284. Steve Kretzmann and Jim Vallette, "Operation Oily Immunity," *CommonDreams.org*, 23 July 2003.
285. Thomas Edsall and Juliet Eilperin, "Lobbyists Set Sights on Money-Making Opportunities in Iraq," *Washington Post*, 2 October 2003.
286. Will Dunham, "U.S. Strives to Privatize Iraqi State-Owned Firms," Reuters, 13 October 2003.
287. Charles Hanley, "US Selling Off Iraq-Owned Companies," Associated Press, 17 October 2003.
288. Rajiv Chandrasekaran, "Attacks Force Retreat From Wide-Ranging Plans for Iraq," *Washington Post*, 28 December 2003.
289. Bacon, op. cit.
290. "U.S. Says Mass Iraq Privatization Still Way Off," Reuters, 10 December 2003.
291. Sue Pleming, "US Drops Iraq Privatization, Focuses on Investors," Reuters, 20 February 2004.
292. Garamone, op.cit.
293. Ken Thomas, "Former Iraq Privatization Official Says Progress Being Made," Associated Press, 27 May 2004.
294. Michael Biesecker, "This Is a New Era in Iraq," *The News & Observer*, 17 January 2004.
295. Ronald Johnson, interview with Naomi Klein, January 2004.
296. James Mayfield's blog posted on the Web site of *Meridian Magazine* at http://www.meridianmagazine.com/exstories/040324iraq.html.
297. John Burns, "There Is No Crash Course in Democracy," *The New York Times*, 14 December 2003.
298. Mayfield blog, op cit
299. Kuhaida interview, op. cit.
300. Michael Hedges and Matt Schwartz, "Ex-Houston Official on the Job in Iraq," *Houston Chronicle*, 15 October 2003.
301. "Houston Barely Avoids Massive Payroll Problem," Associated Press, 30 December 2000.
302. Dan Feldstein, "Pension Rule Changes Aided Top City Officials," *Houston Chronicle*, 3 March 2004 and Doug Miller, "Pension Plan for City Workers Low on Cash," Channel 11 *News*, 3 March 2004.
303. Larry Kaplow, "Selling Iraqis on Benefits of Democracy No Easy Task," *Atlanta Journal-Constitution*, 4 January 2004.
304. Ibrahim Mustafa Hussain, interview with Steve Inskeep, *All Things Considered*, National Public Radio, 20 December 2003.
305. "U.S. Tries Limited Elections in Mosul," *Christian Science Monitor*, 6 May 2003.
306. Nicholas Blanford, "In Iraq's South, Democracy Buds," *Christian Science Monitor*, 16 December 2003.
307. William Booth and Rajiv Chandrasekaran, "Occupation Forces Halt Elections Throughout Iraq," *Washington Post*, 28 June 2003.

308. Johnson interview by Klein, op.cit.

309. Ariana Eunjung Cha, "Hope and Confusion Mark Iraq's Democracy Lessons," *Washington Post*, 24 November 2003.

310. Ibid.

311. Dan Murphy, "Baghdad's Tale of Two Councils," *Christian Science Monitor*, 31 October 2003.

312. Howard LaFranchi, "Democracy From Scratch," *Christian Science Monitor*, 5 December 2003.

313. Ibid.

314. Rory McCarthy, "Doubts Hold Back Rising Star of Iraqi Politics," *Guardian*, 10 February 2004.

315. Ariana Eunjung Cha, "An Iraqi Council With Clout," *Washington Post*, 18 February 2004.

316. Robert Moran, "New Baghdad Mayor Chosen," *Knight Ridder*, 19 April 2004.

317. Jay Price, "RTI Wins Another Contract for Government Creation," *News & Observer*, 1 April 2004.

318. Emily Harris, "Today's Elections to Elect a District Council in Baqubah," *National Public Radio*, 14 February 2004.

319. Herbert Docena, meeting notes from RTI-organized city council meeting.

320. Ibid.

321. Booth and Chandrasekaran, op. cit.

322. Edward Wong, "U.S. Tries to Give Moderates an Edge in Iraqi Elections," *The New York Times*, 18 January 2004.

323. RTI, "Local Governance Project in Iraq,"press release, posted at http://www.rti.org.

324. Jabir Algarawi, interview by author, June 2004.

325. Kuhaida interview, op. cit.

326. Patrick Gibbons, e-mail to author, 2 July 2004.

327. Kuhaida interview, op.cit.

328. Patrick Gibbons, interview by author, June 2004.

329. Ibid

330. *Jane's Defense Weekly*, 11 September 2001.

331. Patrick Cockburn, "The Pretence of an Independent Iraq," *Independent*, 22 June 2004.

332. James Glanz and Erik Eckholm, "Reality Intrudes on Promises in Rebuilding of Iraq," *The New York Times*, 30 June 2004.

333. Rory McCarthy and Jonathan Steele, "Security a Shambles Ahead of Handover," *Guardian*, 24 June 2004.

334. Suzanne Goldenberg, "Iraq Gets Fraction of U.S. Aid Billions," *Guardian*, 5 July 2004.

335. Steven Weisman, "U.S. Is Quietly Spending $2.5 Billion From Iraqi Oil Revenues to Pay for Iraqi Projects," *The New York Times*, 21 June 2004.

Index

231

240 PRATAP CHATTERJEE

Miala, Hamid, 16
Michigan, University of, 168
Microsoft Word, 147
Mikha, Emad, 143
military, 101, 132, 141, 195, 196, 208, 213–14
    British, 134
    contracts, 19 –23, 110
    elections involving U.S., 193–94, 200
    experimenting in war, 9
    financing Halliburton, 29
    outsourcing, 39, 135
    private security similar to, 108
    privatizing, 111
    Professionals Resources Incorporated (MPTR), 135
    training, 139
militias, 121
    forming, 130–31
    private, 131
mining, 119, 134, 137
Ministries
    of Education, 75–76
    of Electricity, 62
    of Health, 85
    of Industry, 181, 182
    Iraqi, 171–75, 183
    of Justice, 171
    of Planning, 12
    of Transportation, 100
mistreatment
    of employees, 26–27
    of prisoners, 148–51
mobile phone towers, 69
Mohamed, Nabel Darwish, 193
Mohammad, Shakir Mahmud, 193
Mohammed, Fakher Fareg, 100
Mohammed, Sa'ad, 80
Mohee, Mohammed, 51, 52
money
    Bechtel wasting, 82
    Islamic transfer system for, 177
    stock piling, 8
Money, Arthur, 139
monopoly, 53, 146
    illegal, 71
Montgomery Ward, 24
Morale Welfare, Recreation (MWR), 30
Morris Corporation, 27
Morris, Ted, 67, 68
Mortenthaler, Jill, 132
mortgaging, oil revenues, 92–95

Mostafa, Saba Adel, 24
Motorola, 108
MSNBC, 166
Muhsin, Abdullah, 19
mujahideen (holy warriors), 8, 126
al Mukhtar, Ghazwan, 123
Mumm, Cliff, 63
Munir Sukhtian, 101
Murray, Craig, 136
Mustafa, Diyar, 142–43
Mustafa, Idris, 142–43

Najibiya power plant, 61
Nakhla, Adel, 148, 151
Naseef, Bakeer, 150
National Cancer Institute, 158
National Ex-servicemen Coordination Committee, 106
National Security Agency, 139, 158, 159–60
National Strategic Policy Studies, 89
National War College, 89
Native Americans, 13, 159
NATO, 144
Natsios, Andrew, 65, 86
Navy, 71, 110, 139
Nazis, 96–97, 132, 155
NBC, 20, 22, 44, 162
Ndebele, Kwa, 120
Nebraska, Omaha, University of (UNO), 84
negotiations, labor, 70
Nelson, Torin, 148, 149–50
New Bridge, 180
news coverage, 8
NEXI, 94
NGO's, 82
    reconstruction work halted by, 90–92
Nicolae, Dumitru, 133
Nightingale, Keith, 158
Nixon, Richard, 14
Noll, Mike, 46
Norcross, Melissa, 23, 25
North, Don, 162, 163
Nour USA, 122
NTC Group, 182
Ntuli, Piet, 120

occupation, 9, 11, 12, 16, 48–52, 69, 72, 73, 77, 131, 154, 163
    anger over, 28

ACKNOWLEDGMENTS

This book is dedicated to the people of Iraq. I truly wish that real democracy and liberation may one day dawn upon your land.

Any mistakes herein are mine alone, and much credit and grateful thanks must go to the many people who risked their lives to tell me their stories, especially those who accompanied me on many foolhardy trips: Gharib, Istifyan, little David, Rana, Thamer, Wadah, Walid, and the staff of Occupation Watch in Baghdad, and those of the Al Fanar and Agadir hotels. I have not disclosed full names for fear that translators and their families would be targets for violence.

I thank my expatriate colleagues who traveled with me on my trips to the regions, David Martinez, Herbert Docena, Aaron Glantz, Naomi Klein and Nobu Sakamoto. Many thanks to the staff of Corpwatch, especially Jennifer Borden, Ben Clarke, Eva Dienel, Tonya Hennessey, Sasha Lilley, David Phinney, Sakura Saunders, and Adam Clay Thompson; our volunteers, Natasha Ott, Harumi Miyazaki and Meinah Sharif; the board, Antonio Diaz, China Brotsky, Antonio Diaz, Josh Karliner and Mele Lau Smith; and our funders, the Lawson Valentine Foundation, the Veatch Foundation, the Lippincott Foundation, the George Washington Williams Fellowship of the Independent Press Association, the Samuel Rubin Foundation, and the Institute for Southern Studies and the Fund for Investigative Journalism.

Much gratitude to the folks at Seven Stories Press especially Greg Ruggiero and Ria Julien, who shepherded this book from the day I started writing to delivery in the book stores in the amazingly short span of five months!

I especially thank the many anonymous whistleblowers who stepped forward at the risk of their careers: the staff of Henry

Waxman and John Dingell, and the long suffering public relations people at the Pentagon, Bechtel, Halliburton, among other companies, who endured my persistent inquiries.

To the dozens of journalists, many of whom I have never met, but whose work I have drawn upon to flesh out my own personal impressions: especially Ariana Eunjung Cha, Rajiv Chandrasekaran, Mary Pat Flaherty, Walter Pincus, Dana Priest, Jackie Spinner, and Jonathan Weisman of the *Washington Post*; Neela Banerjee, Dan Baum, Joel Brinkley, Erik Eckholm, Douglas Jehl, Eric Schmitt, Edward Wong, John Burns, Jeffrey Gettleman, Dexter Filkins, Don Van Natta Jr, and David Unger of *The New York Times*; Dan Murphy, Howard LaFranchi, Nicholas Blanford of the *Christian Science Monitor*; Russell Gold, Neil King, and Chip Cummins at the *Wall Street Journal*; Rob Collier and David Baker at the *San Francisco Chronicle*; Knut Royce of *Newsday*; Scott Shane of the *Baltimore Sun*; T. Christian Miller of the *Los Angeles Times*; Julian Borger and Rory McCarthy of the *Guardian UK*; Matt Kelley at the Associated Press; Sue Pleming at Reuters; Larry Kaplow of Cox News Service; Adam Zagorin at *Time* magazine; Shane Harris of *Government Executive* magazine; David Bacon and Mitch Jeserich of Pacifica Radio; David Enders of *Baghdad Bulletin*; Tucker Carlson at *Esquire*; Seymour Hersh and Jane Mayer at the *New Yorker*; Bob Love and Chip Rowe at *Playboy*; Bruce Bigelow of the *San Diego Union-Tribune*; and Washington DC activists and analysts Doug Brooks, David Isenberg, Peter Singer, Jim Lobe, and Danielle Bryan.

My long standing colleagues and supporters at KPFA radio in Berkeley; Open Society Institute, the World Policy Institute, and *Democracy Now!* in New York; the Institute for Public Accuracy and the Center for Public Integrity in Washington DC; Global Exchange and Code Pink in San Francisco.

Last, but not least, my thanks goes to Elizabeth Sy, for keeping me inspired.